Best Easy Day Hikes
San Fernando Valley

Help Us Keep This Guide Up to Date

Every effort has been made by the author and editors to make this guide as accurate and useful as possible. However, many things can change after a guide is published—trails are rerouted, regulations change, facilities come under new management, etc.

We would love to hear from you concerning your experiences with this guide and how you feel it could be improved and kept up to date. While we may not be able to respond to all comments and suggestions, we'll take them to heart and we'll also make certain to share them with the author. Please send your comments and suggestions to the following address:

Globe Pequot Press
Reader Response/Editorial Department
P.O. Box 480
Guilford, CT 06437

Or you may e-mail us at:

editorial@GlobePequot.com

Thanks for your input, and happy trails!

Best Easy Day Hikes Series

Best Easy Day Hikes
San Fernando Valley

Deke Williams

FALCONGUIDES

GUILFORD, CONNECTICUT
HELENA, MONTANA

AN IMPRINT OF GLOBE PEQUOT PRESS

FALCONGUIDES®

Maps by Off Route Inc. © Morris Book Publishing, LLC
TOPO! Explorer software and SuperQuad source maps courtesy of
National Geographic Maps. For information about TOPO! Explorer,
TOPO!, and Nat Geo Maps products, go to www.topo.com or www
.natgeomaps.com.
Project editor: Julie Marsh
Layout artist: Kevin Mak

Library of Congress Cataloging-in-Publication data
Williams, Deke.
  Best easy day hikes, San Fernando Valley / Deke Williams.
      p. cm. – (FalconGuides)
  ISBN 978-0-7627-5257-7
  1. Hiking–California–San Fernando Valley–Guidebooks. 2. Trails–
California–San Fernando Valley–Guidebooks. 3. San Fernando Valley
(Calif.)–Guidebooks. I. Title.
  GV199.42.C22S268 2009
  917.94'930454–dc22
                                            2009030644

Printed in the United States of America
10 9 8 7 6 5 4 3 2 1

Contents

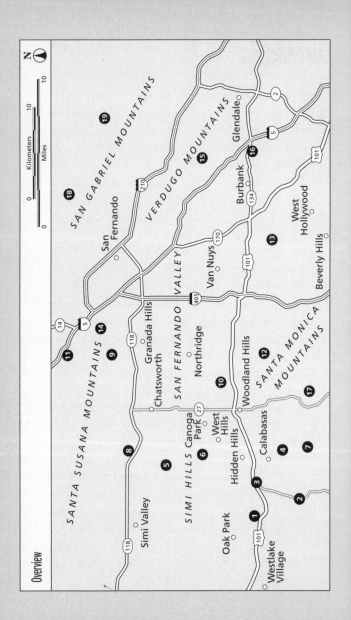

Overview

Introduction

For such an urbanized area, the San Fernando Valley is home to an amazingly large number of outdoor recreational opportunities. Of the many activities enjoyed here, hiking is perhaps the most popular, thanks to favorable year-round weather and an abundance of great hiking areas. With the Valley surrounded by thousands of acres of natural land, excellent hikes are available in just about every direction, and one never needs to drive more than a half hour from the Valley's center to find them.

Helping to make the Valley such an ideal hiking destination is the varied geography of the region. The Santa Monica Mountains form the southern boundary of the Valley, and they alone contain enough worthy hikes to warrant their own separate guidebook. With the inclusion of the Simi Hills to the west, the Santa Susana Mountains to the north, and the San Gabriel and Verdugo Mountains to the north and east, it is no surprise that the San Fernando Valley is the preeminent hub of hiking in Southern California.

Featured within these pages are nineteen of the best easy day hikes in and around the San Fernando Valley. Great hikes within all of the surrounding natural lands have been included, not only to present the diversity of this part of Southern California, but also to provide an introductory sample of each area for those who wish to explore beyond the hikes featured in this book. In keeping with the theme of this guide, all of the hikes are relatively noncommitting and suitable for hikers of all experience levels. All of the hikes were chosen with families in mind, though some have more demanding options available to those looking for more of a challenge.

Weather

The San Fernando Valley is fortunate to have favorable year-round hiking conditions, but there is certainly a time when hiking here is most enjoyable. This time is usually from late winter through spring, though it can extend on either side depending on the weather patterns that year. This season is ideal because mild temperatures and recent rains leave trails dust-free and surrounded by lush vegetation. The air quality is also at its best during this time, meaning you'll breathe easier plus have spectacular views along the way. Sunny days with temperatures in the 60s are the norm during these months, but be sure to check the forecast on the day of your hike and dress accordingly.

Hiking in the summer can be enjoyable as well, but timing your hike during the cooler morning or evening hours is recommended. Midday summer temperatures can reach over 100°F at most of the featured hike locations, so be sure to carry extra water if you must hike during this time. You should also get acclimated to the hot weather by beginning with short, easy hikes in the heat before attempting any longer or more challenging ones. Hot weather can make even the easiest hike in this book a taxing test of survival if you are not prepared.

Land Management

Besides the great weather, the San Fernando Valley is fortunate to have many organizations working toward the maintenance and preservation of the surrounding wildlands. These are not easy tasks, considering that the Valley is one of the most populated areas in the United States, and the surrounding natural lands are constantly under threat from overuse and encroaching development.

The most renowned of these organizations is the Santa Monica Mountains Conservancy, which oversees the area and helps to acquire and preserve land for outdoor recreation. The majority of hikes in this book fall under the management of this group, or one of their affiliates, and a few restrictions apply to their land. Generally, the parklands are closed from sunset until sunrise, and they do not allow smoking, fires, alcoholic beverages, littering, unauthorized vehicle use, or the damaging or defacing of property. Exceptions or additional restrictions are usually listed at the trailhead information kiosks located near the parking areas for each hike.

Two of the hikes featured in this book take place within the Angeles National Forest, where fewer restrictions are in place. Contact the ranger's office to learn the specific restrictions for these hikes and to obtain an Adventure Pass, which is required to park at certain areas within the national forest. Contact information can be found in the specs for each hike.

As the manager of the Santa Monica Mountains National Recreation Area, which includes the Cheeseboro Canyon hike in this book, the National Park Service deserves mention here as well. The SMMNRA is the world's largest urban national park, comprising 153,075 acres. Devoted to preserving, restoring, and learning from the land, the NPS has had their work cut out for them since becoming involved in the area in 1978. Their Visitor Center, located in Thousand Oaks, has many historic and cultural exhibits on display, making it a worthwhile stop if you are in the area. Visit www.nps.gov/samo for more information.

Getting into Shape

Unless you want to be sore—and possibly have to shorten your trip or vacation—be sure to get in shape before a big hike. If you're terribly out of shape, start a walking program early, preferably eight weeks in advance. Start with a fifteen-minute walk during your lunch hour or after work and gradually increase your walking time to an hour. You should also increase your elevation gain. Walking briskly up hills really strengthens your leg muscles and gets your heart rate up. If you work in a storied office building, take the stairs instead of the elevator. If you prefer going to a gym, walk the treadmill or use a stair machine. You can further increase your strength and endurance by walking with a loaded backpack. Stationary exercises you might consider are squats, leg lifts, sit-ups, and push-ups. Other good ways to get in shape include biking, running, aerobics, and, of course, short hikes. Stretching before and after a hike keeps muscles flexible and helps avoid injuries.

Hiking with Children

Hiking with children is all about seeing and experiencing nature through their eyes. Kids like to explore and have fun. They like to stop and point out bugs and plants, look under rocks, jump in puddles, and throw sticks. If you're taking a toddler or young child on a hike, start with a trail that you're familiar with. Trails that have interesting things for kids, like piles of leaves to play in or a small stream to wade through during the summer, will make the hike much more enjoyable for them and will keep them from getting bored.

You can keep your child's attention if you have a strategy before starting on the trail. Using games is not only an effective way to keep a child involved, it's also a great way to teach him or her about nature. Play hide and seek, where your child is the mouse and you are the hawk. Quiz children on the names of plants and animals. If your children are old enough, let them carry their own daypacks filled with snacks and water. So that you are sure to go at their pace and not yours, let them lead the way. Playing follow the leader works particularly well when you have a group of children. Have each child take a turn at being the leader.

Hiking with Dogs

Bringing your furry friend with you is always more fun than leaving him behind. Our canine pals make great trail buddies because they never complain and always make good company.

Before you plan outdoor adventures with your dog, make sure he's in shape for the trail. Take him on your daily runs or walks. Also, be sure he has a firm grasp of the basics of canine etiquette and behavior, and that he can sit, lie down, stay, and come on command. Purchase collapsible water and dog food bowls for your dog. If you are hiking on rocky terrain or in the snow, you can purchase footwear for your dog that will protect his feet from cuts and bruises.

Once on the trail, keep your dog under control. You can buy a flexi-lead that allows your dog to go exploring along the trail, while allowing you the ability to reel him in should another hiker approach or should he decide to chase a rabbit. Always obey leash laws and be sure to bury your dog's waste or pack it in resealable plastic bags.

Water

Even in frigid conditions, you need at least two quarts of water a day to function efficiently. Add heat and taxing terrain and you can bump that figure up to one gallon. That's simply a base to work from—your metabolism and your level of conditioning can raise or lower that amount. Unless you know your level, assume that you need one gallon of water a day. Now, where do you plan on getting the water?

The easiest solution is to bring water with you. Natural water sources can be loaded with intestinal disturbers, such as bacteria, viruses, and fertilizers. *Giardia lamblia,* the most common of these disturbers, is a protozoan parasite that lives part of its life cycle as a cyst in water sources. The parasite spreads when mammals defecate in water sources. Once ingested, *Giardia* can induce cramping, diarrhea, vomiting, and fatigue within two days to two weeks after ingestion. If you believe you've contracted giardiasis, see a doctor immediately, as it is treatable with prescription drugs.

Dehydration

Have you ever hiked in hot weather and had a roaring headache and felt fatigued after only a few miles? More than likely you were dehydrated. Symptoms of dehydration include fatigue, headache, and decreased coordination and judgment. When you are hiking, your body's rate of fluid loss depends on the outside temperature, humidity, altitude, and your activity level. On average, a hiker walking in warm weather will lose four liters of fluid a day. That fluid loss is easily replaced by normal consumption of liquids and food. However, if a hiker is walking briskly in hot, dry weather and hauling a heavy pack, he or she can lose one to three liters of water an hour. It's important to always carry plenty of water and to stop often and drink fluids regularly, even if you aren't thirsty.

Hazards

Besides heat-related danger, there are a few other safety issues relevant to hiking around the San Fernando Valley. First and foremost is the presence of poison oak at almost half of the hikes featured in this book. This nuisance is easily avoided once you know what to look for. The plant usually grows in a dense shrub along damp, shady areas. Its telltale leaves are composed of three leaflets that have a glossy, dark green appearance, which can change to red or pink depending on the season. Contact with the plant causes skin irritation among most people, with constant itching leading to small blisters or lesions that will clear up after about ten days. The best defense against this irritant is to wear clothing that covers the arms, legs, and torso. There are also nonprescription lotions you can apply to exposed skin that guard against the effects of poison oak. Should you come in contact with the plant, wash the affected area thoroughly with soap and cold water, and consult your doctor if you experience severe irritation or swelling.

Another hazard that can be found within all the hiking areas featured in this book is rattlesnakes. Identified by their triangular heads and the rattles on their tails, they sport various shades of brown and black stripes. They are commonly seen during the warmer months, usually stretched across a trail soaking up the heat of the sun. Unless they feel threatened, rattlesnakes are not aggressive, so simply be on the

the lookout for them and steer clear if you spot one. Should you get bitten, remain calm and get to a hospital as soon as possible. Do not apply a tourniquet to the bite area or try to suck out the venom with your mouth.

More of an annoyance than a direct hazard, ticks are also common along all the hikes in this book. Most abundant during the spring, these crafty arthropods crawl up onto the grasses and bushes that line trails, and cling to you as you brush past. Their small size can make them hard to spot, but wearing light-colored clothing can make it easier to detect their dark brown bodies. Ticks are known carriers of Lyme disease and Rocky Mountain spotted fever, although it is rare for someone in California to become afflicted with either from a tick bite. If you find that one has attached itself onto your skin, use tweezers to grasp the head as close to your skin as possible and pull it straight out. Clean the affected area with an antibacterial cleanser and then apply triple antibiotic ointment. Be sure to monitor the area for a few days. If a part of the tick remains embedded, or if a rash develops around the area, consult your doctor as soon as possible. Also, if hiking with a dog, be sure to check it for ticks as well.

Zero Impact

Like the freeways, the trails in and around the San Fernando Valley see a lot of traffic. To keep these valuable assets enjoyable for everyone, please keep the following in mind:

- Do not litter, period. Consider taking the extra step and pick up trash left by those less considerate.
- Do not approach or feed wildlife.
- Leave the trail and surroundings in their natural state.

- Do not cut switchbacks. The seconds you save can scar the land for years.
- Be courteous to other trail users.
- Come to the trail prepared. This includes taking care of bodily needs before you arrive.

How to Use This Book

This book is designed to be a simple and straightforward guide to the best easy day hikes in and around the San Fernando Valley. Each featured hike includes a map of the trail, directions to the trailhead, and a summary of what makes the hike special. The specifics of the hike are also included, such as the length, difficulty, whether any fees or permits are required, canine compatibility, contact information, and the hours during which the trail is open. Lastly, a detailed route-finder explains how to navigate the trail and includes the mileages between important landmarks and junctions.

Difficulty Ratings

The hikes featured in this book have been chosen with beginning hikers in mind. Attempts have been made to keep most of the routes below a certain commitment level, meaning that you have the option of turning around early, with the return trip being easier than the way in. The ratings for each hike are from the perspective of a beginning hiker, and are mostly clues as to the length and amount of climbing involved. Keep in mind that these ratings are subjective and vulnerable to outside factors such as weather or changing trail conditions.

- **Easy** hikes generally have minimal elevation gain or loss, and can be completed in less than two hours when hiking at a leisurely pace.
- **Moderate** hikes tend to involve either sustained yet gradual climbs or short but steep climbs, mixed with

easier terrain. These hikes usually take two to four hours to complete.

- **More challenging** hikes feature steep and sustained climbing, usually for an hour or more. Only a few of the hikes in this book carry this rating.

Trail Finder

Best Hikes for Children

Best Hikes for Dogs

Best Hikes for Nature Lovers

Best Hikes for Great Views

Map Legend

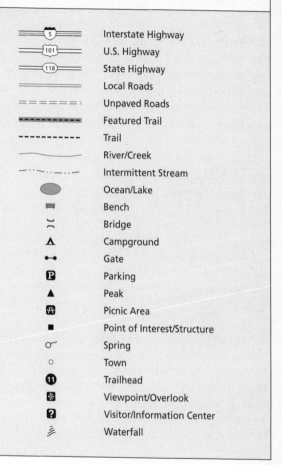

5	Interstate Highway
101	U.S. Highway
118	State Highway
	Local Roads
	Unpaved Roads
	Featured Trail
	Trail
	River/Creek
	Intermittent Stream
	Ocean/Lake
	Bench
	Bridge
	Campground
	Gate
P	Parking
	Peak
	Picnic Area
	Point of Interest/Structure
	Spring
	Town
11	Trailhead
	Viewpoint/Overlook
?	Visitor/Information Center
	Waterfall

1 Cheeseboro Canyon Trail

Located among the rolling hills that separate the San Fernando and Conejo Valleys, Cheeseboro Canyon is an ideal place for day hiking. This pleasant hike takes you through pastoral meadows and shady oak groves to the head of the historic canyon. With several unique features and an abundance of trails, this is an area that you will want to visit again and again.

Distance: 8.2 miles out and back
Approximate hiking time: 4 hours
Best season: Oct–May
Difficulty: Moderate due to distance
Trail surface: Well-traveled dirt road or trail
Other users: Equestrians and mountain bikers

Canine compatibility: Leashed dogs permitted
Fees and permits: None required
Schedule: Always open
Map: USGS Calabasas, CA
Trail contact: Santa Monica Mountains National Recreation Area; (805) 370-2301

Finding the trailhead: From the Valley, take US 101 west to the Chesebro Road exit. Turn right at the stop sign and head north on Palo Comado Canyon Road. At the next stop sign, turn right (north) onto Chesebro Road. After 0.7 mile, you will reach the lower parking area, located on the right at the intersection of Cheeseboro Canyon Road. Many people park here, but the main parking area is 0.2 mile farther up Cheeseboro Canyon Road. GPS N34 9.365'/W118 43.870'

The Hike

Equally rich in history and natural beauty, Cheeseboro Canyon is a wonderful place to visit. For thousands of years the Native American Chumash people called this area home, and they established many of the trails still in use today. The land was later used extensively for cattle ranching, resulting in the barren hillsides that surround the lower part of the canyon. After the native plant population was decimated by the grazing cattle, ranchers planted nonnative wild oats, mustard, and thistle to better suit the needs of heavy grazing. This went on for over 150 years, and although it was not a natural process, it has given the canyon a unique look that is particularly striking in the spring.

In addition to its historical value, Cheeseboro Canyon is home to a variety of animals, and there is a good chance of seeing coyotes, deer, or birds of prey along this trail. In fact, the canyon has the largest concentration of birds of prey nesting sites in the Lower 48, so their presence is almost guaranteed. Absent from the canyon, however, are the grizzly bears that once thrived here, having been killed off long ago by the cattle ranchers.

While the featured hike can be enjoyed year-round, it is most beautiful during the late winter/early spring months, when the hills are carpeted with lush green grass and the stream is flowing steadily. During the summer the area is notoriously hot, so be sure to carry extra water and avoid hiking in the middle of the day. Much of the lower canyon is shaded with giant Valley oak trees, so summer hiking can be enjoyable as long as you are prepared for the heat.

At the bottom half of the canyon, the trail is mostly a well-traveled dirt road, following a leisurely route that stays in the oak-shaded canyon. A little after 3 miles, the road narrows to trail as you enter the Sulphur Springs area. The "fragrance" in the air will confirm that you have reached the springs as you cross the creek and climb alongside it. After heavy rains, the creek takes on a milky hue from all

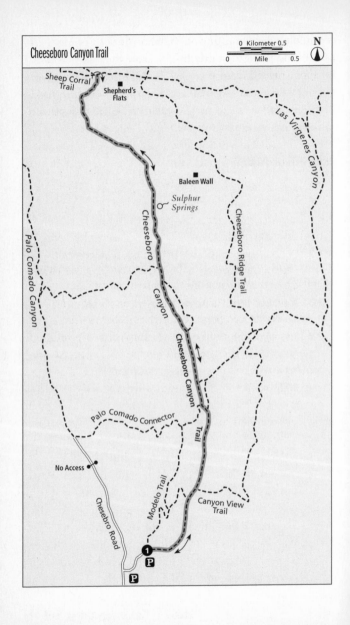

Cheeseboro Canyon Trail

Sheep Corral Trail

Shepherd's Flats

Baleen Wall

Sulphur Springs

Cheeseboro Canyon

Las Virgenes Canyon

Cheeseboro Ridge Trail

Palo Comado Canyon

Cheeseboro Canyon Trail

Palo Comado Connector

No Access

Cheseboro Road

Modelo Trail

Canyon View Trail

1

P

P

0   Kilometer   0.5

0   Mile   0.5

N

the sulphur leeching into it. Sulphur Springs is a popular turnaround point for many hikers, since the trail becomes a bit more rugged from there on. Several short, steep climbs littered with rocks await those who continue to Shepherd's Flats, but the views of the Baleen Wall rock formation to the east make the effort worthwhile.

Miles and Directions

0.0 Begin at the trailhead on the east side of main parking area. The trail is the dirt road heading east.

0.7 At the junction with the Canyon View Trail, stay on main road as it heads north.

1.3 Dirt road splits in two, with the right fork leading to the Cheeseboro Ridge Trail and the Baleen Wall. Instead, follow the left fork to stay on the Cheeseboro Canyon Trail.

1.9 A dirt road heads to the right. Instead, go straight on the smaller dirt road, which soon becomes a narrow trail.

2.3 Trail rejoins the dirt road. Keep heading north on the road.

3.1 Sulphur Springs section is reached. The trail crosses the stream—no bridge here—and ascends next to it. This is a good spot to turn around if you are feeling tired or would like a shorter hike.

4.1 Trail concludes at Shepherd's Flats, with three smaller trails branching off in different directions. This is the end of the featured hike. Return the way you came.

8.2 Hike finishes at the main parking lot.

2 Malibu Creek State Park Backcountry Trails

Escape the crowds that flock to Malibu Creek State Park with this fun loop of lesser-known backcountry trails. The moderate trails featured here wind their way through shaded oak and redwood groves, and pass by the tranquil shores of Century Lake. Altogether they create one of the most scenic hikes in this book.

Distance: 3.1-mile lollipop
Approximate hiking time: 2 hours
Best season: Sept–June
Difficulty: Moderate, with some short climbs toward the end
Trail surface: Well-traveled dirt trails or dirt road
Other users: Equestrians; mountain bikers on Crags Road

Canine compatibility: Dogs not allowed on trails within the state park
Fees and permits: None
Schedule: Dawn to dusk
Map: USGS Malibu Beach, CA
Trail contact: Malibu Creek State Park; (818) 880-0367

Finding the trailhead: From the Valley, take US 101 west toward Ventura. Exit at Las Virgenes Road and head south for roughly 3.5 miles, where you make a right on Mulholland Highway. After 1.7 miles on Mulholland, be on the lookout for a wide dirt pullout on the left, with a couple of 4-foot-high utility boxes in the middle of it. You are looking for the Cistern Trail, but the sign is hard to see when traveling west on Mulholland. If you see the sign for the Phantom Trail on your right, you have just passed the Cistern Trail by 300 feet. GPS N34 6.317'/W118 43.909'

The Hike

Malibu Creek State Park is the premier outdoor getaway in the Santa Monica Mountains. Visitors from all over Southern California arrive daily to explore the idyllic valleys and meadows and to take in the numerous attractions offered by the park. First-time visitors are usually astonished to see such wilderness so close to the city, and even those who have been there many times can still discover something new within the park. With the availability of great hiking and equestrian trails, excellent mountain bike rides, and demanding rock-climbing routes, it is not hard to see why Malibu Creek State Park is so popular.

Before being purchased by the state in 1974, the park's land was owned by the 20th Century-Fox movie studio. Many films and television shows, such as *Tarzan, Planet of the Apes,* and *M*A*S*H,* were filmed here. The *M*A*S*H* filming location, evidenced by a couple of rusted jeep bodies, is still a popular hiking destination.

Most people access the park from the main entrance (fee required) located off Malibu Canyon Road, just south of Mulholland Highway. A large parking area, restrooms, and information kiosks are located there. If it is your first visit to the park and you would like an easy introduction to the hiking in the area, it may be worth entering there and taking a stroll along Crags Road to the visitor center (open on weekends) and the Rock Pool.

The featured hike begins west of the main entrance along Mulholland Highway, far away from the crowds. There is no fee to park here, but the area is less secure, so

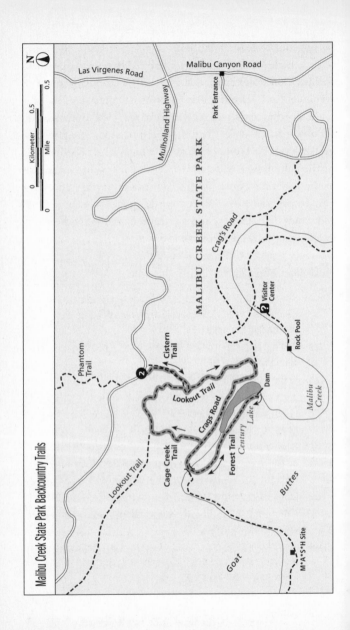

Malibu Creek State Park Backcountry Trails

N

0   0.5   Kilometer
0   0.5   Mile

Las Virgenes Road

Malibu Canyon Road

Mulholland Highway

Park Entrance

MALIBU CREEK STATE PARK

Phantom Trail

Cistern Trail

Lookout Trail

Crag's Road

Visitor Center

Rock Pool

Lookout Trail

Cage Creek Trail

Crags Road

Dam

Century Lake

Forest Trail

Malibu Creek

Buttes

Goat

M*A*S*H Site

be sure not to leave tempting valuables within view inside your vehicle. A few other cars will likely be parked at the trailhead on weekends, but most of the time during the week you will have the place to yourself. Compared to the wide, flat dirt roads that start from the park's main entrance, the route featured here is rugged and narrow from the get-go, making for more enjoyable hiking. With the first half of the hike being mostly downhill or flat, you also arrive at the beautiful Forest Trail much more quickly, affording you extra time to mosey among the giant oaks and coast redwoods that shade this fern-lined trail. It makes the mildly challenging return trip worth every drop of sweat.

Miles and Directions

0.0 From the dirt parking area along Mulholland Highway, the Cistern Trail heads briefly uphill to its namesake before descending the ridge.

0.3 Trail arrives at the Lookout Trail; head left (south) to continue the descent.

0.4 Crags Road is reached. Bear right onto this wide dirt road.

0.5 A dirt road heads south to Century Lake. There is a great picnic area 0.2 mile down this road, but for our route, keep going straight on Crags Road.

1.0 Cage Creek Trail is passed on the right. This trail will be used for the return trip, so take note of its location. For now, continue straight.

1.1 Crags Road crosses Malibu Creek on a wide concrete bridge. Immediately after crossing, bear left onto an unmarked dirt trail. This is the Forest Trail.

1.3 After meandering under large oak trees, even larger coast redwoods are encountered along the trail, as well as some interesting volcanic rock formations.

1.6 Forest Trail ends at the Century Lake dam. Turn around here, and retrace your steps back to Crags Road. Follow road back to the Cage Creek Trail.

2.2 Turn left onto the Cage Creek Trail.

2.5 Cage Creek Trail ends at the Lookout Trail in a large meadow. Head right (east) onto this trail.

2.9 Cistern Trail is reached, thus completing the loop. Turn left and follow the trail back to the parking area.

3.1 The hike concludes at the parking area along Mulholland Highway.

3 Anza Loop Trail to Calabash Canyon Loop Trail

Similar to Cheeseboro Canyon, the Anza Loop Trail offers a convenient way to access the rolling, grass-covered hills that lie between the San Fernando and Conejo Valleys. While the nearby freeway can be a bit noisy, the historic value of this trail more than makes up for the distraction. When combined with the tranquility of the Calabash Canyon Loop Trail, the two trails add up to one excellent hike.

Distance: 2.8-mile lollipop
Approximate hiking time: 1.5 hours
Best season: Nov–April
Difficulty: Easy
Trail surface: Well-traveled dirt trail; can become overgrown in places during late spring/summer
Other users: Equestrians and mountain bikers

Canine compatibility: Leashed dogs permitted
Fees and permits: None required
Schedule: Sunrise to sunset
Map: USGS Calabasas, CA
Trail contact: Santa Monica Mountains Conservancy; (310) 589-3200

Finding the trailhead: From the San Fernando Valley, take US 101 west. Exit at Las Virgenes Road and head south. After you pass over the freeway, turn left at the first stop light onto the unmarked Romdell Road, which turns into a dirt road after 50 feet. Follow the dirt road up to the bottom of the obvious canyon, where it ends at a small dirt parking area next to the trailhead kiosk. GPS N34 8.794'/W118 41.781'

The Hike

The Juan Bautista de Anza Trail bears the name of the famous Spanish explorer and commemorates the route taken by him and his party in 1776 on their way to establish a mission in northern California. Along the trail are several informative displays; some depict the historical significance of the route, while others point out the diverse vegetation of the area.

The hike described here omits a good portion of the Juan Bautista de Anza Trail in favor of the Anza Loop Trail, which is used to connect to the Calabash Canyon Loop Trail. The omitted section of trail runs right next to the incessantly noisy US 101, but it is worth checking out if you want to learn more about the area. One of the attractions along this trail is a hundred-year-old section of pavement that was once part of El Camino Real, the 600-mile-long mission-connecting route that extended from San Diego to Sonoma.

After turning onto the Anza Loop Trail, you will climb a few switchbacks before traversing a hillside. This section of trail is narrow and, depending on the time of year, may be a bit overgrown. After a short while it connects with a dirt road, which will take you up to the Calabash Canyon Loop Trail. This trail starts off on an exposed grassy hillside but eventually makes its way into a wooded canyon after crossing an intermittent stream. Much work is under way to restore this part of the canyon to its natural state, and certain features are being added that will help the native plant and animal populations thrive.

Heading down the canyon in a pleasant oak-shaded corridor, you follow a perennial seep until the trail intersects

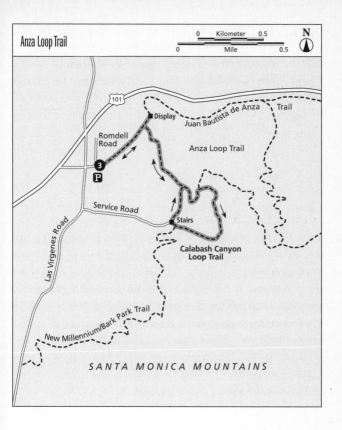

the top of a long staircase made of railroad ties. Climb down these stairs carefully, and bear right when you reach the dirt road below. After a short climb up the road, you return to the intersection of the Anza Loop Trail. Retrace this trail back to the Juan Bautista de Anza Trail, then down the canyon to the parking area.

Miles and Directions

0.0 Begin at the dirt parking area at the Juan Bautista de Anza trailhead.

0.3 Reach the signed turnoff for the Anza Loop Trail on the right. Before turning, continue a few hundred feet farther down the Juan Bautista de Anza Trail to an informative display that overlooks the freeway. Return to the turnoff after viewing the display.

0.4 Back at the turnoff for the Anza Loop Trail, follow it south as it switchbacks a few times and traverses the hillside.

0.8 Arrive at a dirt road. Head left to continue on the Anza Loop Trail.

1.0 Turn right at the intersection of the Calabash Canyon Loop Trail, following this trail as it descends into the canyon.

1.9 Arrive at a long staircase at the intersection with the New Millennium/Bark Park Trail. Descend the steps carefully, and turn right onto the dirt road at the bottom.

2.1 Loop is completed as you arrive back at the Anza Loop Trail. Turn left and retrace your steps back toward the parking area.

2.4 Turn left onto Juan Bautista de Anza Trail.

2.8 Hike concludes at the Juan Bautista de Anza trailhead.

4 Calabasas Cold Creek Trail

Once known as the Secret Trail, the Calabasas Cold Creek Trail has the feel of a remote backcountry path, while being only minutes from the Valley. The trail twists through scrub oak groves, chaparral, and sandstone towers, rising gradually until it ends at the Calabasas Peak Motorway. From there, less than a mile's trek lands you atop the proud summit of Calabasas Peak.

Distance: 4.2 miles out and back
Approximate hiking time: 3 hours
Best season: Oct–May
Difficulty: Moderate
Trail surface: Well-traveled dirt trail; may be overgrown in parts during the spring/summer
Other users: Equestrians and mountain bikers

Canine compatibility: Leashed dogs permitted
Fees and permits: None required
Schedule: Sunrise to sunset
Map: USGS Malibu Beach, CA
Trail contact: Santa Monica Mountains Conservancy; (310) 589-3200

Finding the trailhead: From US 101, exit at Valley Circle Boulevard and head south for 1 mile until you reach Val Mar. Make a right onto Val Mar and continue until you intersect Mulholland Highway. Turn right onto Mulholland Highway and drive just over 2 miles. Look for a large dirt parking area on the left (south) side of the highway, a few hundred feet past the Mountain Park Estates gated community. The trailhead and sign are visible from the highway. GPS N34 7.592'/W118 39.442'

The Hike

Hiking the Calabasas Cold Creek Trail provides a convenient way to experience the best of what the Santa Monica

Mountains have to offer. The trail meanders through shady scrub oak groves, over tranquil streams, and around sandstone rock formations, with the added bonus of leading the day hiker to the top of Calabasas Peak, elevation 2,163 feet. All of this takes place in an area considered to be a vital wildlife-access corridor, so the chances of spotting some of the native fauna are pretty good.

The trail is most enjoyable during the cooler months, when the hills and valleys are seas of green. Come spring and summer, the trail becomes overgrown in a few sections with mustard weed and sow thistle. If hiking during these warmer months, be on the lookout for ticks, as the tall vegetation can make it easy for them to brush off onto you or your dog.

About a quarter of the way into the hike, some exposure is encountered as the trail climbs up several steep switchbacks. Although the footing is good, the trail becomes narrower as it scales the hillside, culminating at an airy perch overlooking the valley below. Past this excellent viewing area, the trail follows the ridge up, with a few more switchbacks to contend with. The sight of all the nearby tract housing developments can obscure the natural beauty of the area, so focus your attention instead on the numerous sandstone rock formations, which become visible as the trail begins to top out. These slabs of cemented sand were once part of a large layer of sedimentary rock beneath the ocean. Now their outcroppings serve as nesting spots for birds of prey.

When the trail ends at the Calabasas Peak Motorway, turn right onto this wide dirt road to begin the moderate climb toward Calabasas Peak. When the road flattens out at the top of the ridge, Calabasas Peak will be to the right

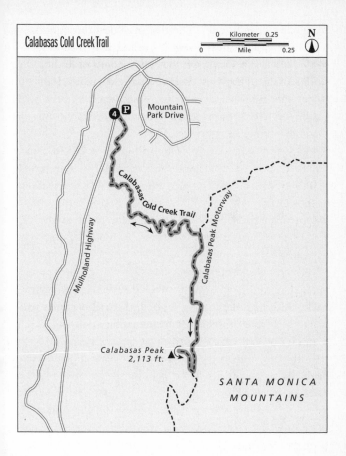

Mountain
Park Drive

Calabasas Cold Creek Trail

Calabasas Peak Motorway

Mulholland Highway

Calabasas Peak
2,113 ft.

SANTA MONICA
MOUNTAINS

(west). Follow a faint trail up the left spine of the road cut
to a saddle, then head through the chaparral to the summit.
Once there, take time to sign the peak register, and enjoy
the panoramic views of the San Fernando Valley, the Conejo
Valley, Los Angeles, and the ocean. Having attained all the
elevation you can, the return trip is almost all downhill; just
retrace your steps back to the highway.

Miles and Directions

0.0   Begin at the parking area on Mulholland Highway.

0.8   Calabasas Cold Creek Trail begins ascending several steep switchbacks.

1.2   Trail ends at Calabasas Peak Motorway. Head right on this dirt road.

2.0   Look for a faint trail on the right leading up the left edge of the road cut. Follow it up to the saddle.

2.1   Summit of Calabasas Peak. Return the way you came, taking care on the loose sections.

4.2   Arrive back at the trailhead.

5 Sage Ranch Loop Trail

Located atop the Simi Hills, the Sage Ranch Loop Trail offers a scenic tour of the sandstone rock formations typical of the area and provides excellent views of the San Fernando and Simi Valleys. The loop has minimal climbing, making this hike a perfect outing for the whole family.

Distance: 2.5-mile loop
Approximate hiking time: 1.5 hours
Best season: Oct–June
Difficulty: Easy
Trail surface: Well-traveled dirt road
Other users: Equestrians and mountain bikers

Canine compatibility: Leashed dogs permitted
Fees and permits: None required
Schedule: Sunrise to sunset
Map: USGS Calabasas, CA
Trail contact: Sage Ranch Ranger Station; (310) 999-3753

Finding the trailhead: From CA 118, take Topanga Canyon Boulevard south. Turn right on Plummer and follow it to the intersection with Box Canyon Road, veering left (south) onto Valley Circle. At the intersection with Woolsey Canyon Road, turn right. Head up Woolsey Canyon until it ends at Black Canyon Road, and turn right. The entrance to Sage Ranch Park is about 0.2 mile north of the intersection, on the left. GPS N34 14.467'/W118 40.324'

The Hike

High atop the rugged, boulder-strewn Simi Hills, Sage Ranch feels relatively remote, despite its accessibility and close proximity to the Valley. These qualities attracted early filmmakers, who used the area as a backdrop for hundreds of Westerns beginning in the 1930s. The isolated setting also drew the U.S. government to the area, for it was an ideal location to test nuclear reactors and rocket engines. The Santa Susana Field Laboratory was established here in the mid-1940s and was later known as Rocketdyne. Unfortunately, the experiments performed at the facility did not always go as planned, and several incidents caused severe damage to the environment. Many cleanup and containment efforts have since been initiated and, thankfully, hiking in neighboring Sage Ranch does not pose a health risk.

From the main parking area just off Black Canyon Road, the hike begins by climbing a short segment of paved road before topping out at the upper parking area. A portable toilet and trail information can be found here. At the north end of the upper parking area, the trail heads into a grove of oak trees. There are many unmarked trails that lead to various rock formations and lookouts, and if you have extra time, they may be worth exploring. To stay on the Loop Trail, be sure to follow the arrows painted on the wooden posts planted at the intersections of these trails.

After weaving around many sandstone crags and contending with some short climbs, you will pass Turtle Rock on the right at 0.9 mile. This large sandstone formation sits at the crest of the hill, overlooking Simi Valley, and is an excellent spot to stop and have lunch. After Turtle Rock, the trail begins its descent into a small valley and is soon bordered by property once used by Rocketdyne and the Santa Susana Field Laboratory. Be sure to heed any warnings about entering this property, as it is potentially unsafe to do so. Instead, stay on the main trail as it heads east, gently rising toward Black Canyon Road. Once the trail turns northward, it winds around a few more boulders before ending at the parking area.

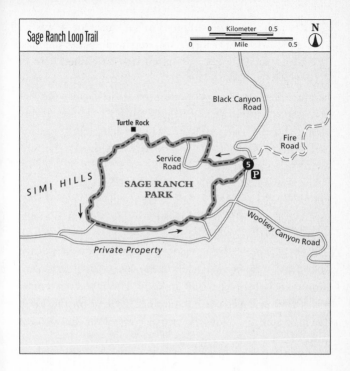

Miles and Directions

0.0 Beginning at the parking area off Black Canyon Road, head uphill on the paved road.

0.3 Paved road ends at the upper parking area (normally closed to parking). From the north end of the parking area, follow the dirt road into the oak grove.

0.9 Trail passes Turtle Rock on the right.

1.5 Trail drops down into a small valley and begins heading east, paralleling private property.

2.5 Loop finishes at southern end of parking area.

6 Upper Las Virgenes Canyon Open Space Preserve

Enjoyable hiking over rolling, grass-covered hills awaits those who visit the Upper Las Virgenes Canyon Open Space Preserve. Rich with history, the preserve signifies the victorious outcome of a hard-fought struggle against the land-development project known as Ahmanson Ranch. This hike is a loop composed of four different trails that combine to offer a great introduction to the area and is suitable for the whole family.

Distance: 3.7-mile lollipop
Approximate hiking time: 2 hours
Best season: Oct–June
Difficulty: Easy, with one gradual, sustained climb
Trail surface: Well-traveled dirt road
Other users: Equestrians and mountain bikers

Canine compatibility: Leashed dogs permitted
Fees and permits: Small fee to park at the trailhead
Schedule: Sunrise to sunset
Map: USGS Calabasas, CA
Trail contact: Santa Monica Mountains Conservancy; (310) 589-3200

Finding the trailhead: From US 101, take Valley Circle Boulevard north approximately 2.5 miles to Victory Boulevard. Turn left onto Victory and follow it several blocks until it ends at the parking area for the Upper Las Virgenes Canyon Open Space Preserve. There is a small fee to park at the trailhead, or you can park for free alongside Victory Boulevard, about 500 feet before the trailhead parking lot. GPS N34 11.107'/W118 40.090'

The Hike

The Upper Las Virgenes Canyon Open Space Preserve is an area of major significance, both historically as well as in what the preserve represents today. Once the domain of the Native American Chumash people, the area was home to at least one major settlement. Many sacred and cultural sites can be found in the surrounding hills, such as Castle Peak and the Cave of Munits, which lie a short distance to the north in El Escorpion Park. By the late 1700s the land belonged to Spanish colonists and was part of the 113,000-acre Rancho San Jose de Gracias de Simi. Beginning in the early 1900s, the land was used for filming many high-profile movies, including *Gone with the Wind* and *They Died with Their Boots On*, as well as dozens of television shows and commercials.

In 1963 the land was purchased by the H. F. Ahmanson Company for the purpose of building a large residential subdivision. The project never got off the ground, but it remained an ongoing threat to the area. Known as Ahmanson Ranch, plans for the area became more ambitious by 1983, when a planned community was proposed for construction atop Laskey Mesa and the surrounding hills. The plan was met with great opposition from many different groups, who called for the preservation of the entire area. Victory was theirs in 2003, when the Ahmanson Ranch property was bought by the Santa Monica Mountains Conservancy, and the area was dedicated as public parkland on April 10, 2004.

It is fortunate that the area was spared from development because it is home to several endangered or sensitive species of plants and animals. The San Fernando Valley spine-

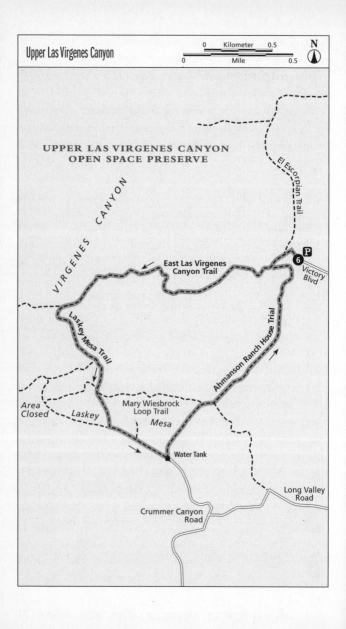

Kilometer

Mile

N

UPPER LAS VIRGENES CANYON
OPEN SPACE PRESERVE

VIRGENES CANYON

El Escorpian Trail

East Las Virgenes
Canyon Trail

P
6
Victory Blvd

Laskey Mesa Trail

Ahmanson Ranch House Trial

Area
Closed

Laskey

Mesa

Mary Wiesbrock
Loop Trail

Water Tank

Long Valley
Road

Crummer Canyon
Road

flower can be found atop Laskey Mesa, where it exists as one of only two known populations in the world. Also, the endangered California red-legged frog resides in pools along East Las Virgenes Creek. Many consider this population to be the only hope this species has for survival, now that their home is under protection. Keep this in mind as you hike along East Las Virgenes Canyon and atop Laskey Mesa, and be sure to not disturb any of the signed sensitive areas.

Miles and Directions

0.0 Hike begins at the trailhead kiosk on the north side of the Victory trailhead parking area. From here, head southwest on the well-traveled dirt road.

0.1 Dirt road arrives at a T. Bear right to head downhill on the East Las Virgenes Canyon Trail.

1.2 Veer left at the fork, and head downhill on the Laskey Mesa Trail.

1.9 After climbing for 0.5 mile, veer right after a sharp left turn in the road to head south onto Laskey Mesa. You are now on the Mary Wiesbrock Loop Trail.

2.1 Dirt road intersects a wider dirt road. Turn left to continue the loop.

2.4 Arrive at a silver water tank surrounded by a few deserted buildings. The loop trail continues left, heading northeast.

2.7 Mary Wiesbrock Loop Trail turns off to the left. Instead, bear right to merge onto the Ahmanson Ranch House Trail. After a few hundred feet, veer left at the fork with the dirt portion of Long Valley Road.

3.6 Arrive back at the East Las Virgenes Canyon Trail. Turn right and retrace it back to the trailhead.

3.7 Arrive back at the parking area.

7 Stunt High Trail to Cold Creek Valley Preserve

Stroll along year-round Cold Creek and explore Native American artifacts on this exceptional hike that the whole family will enjoy. Located in one of the most biologically diverse, yet accessible, watersheds in the Santa Monica Mountains, this hike will give you a better appreciation of the historical and natural features of the area.

Distance: 2.4-mile lollipop
Approximate hiking time: 1.5 hours
Best season: Sept–June
Difficulty: Easy
Trail surface: Well-traveled dirt trail; occasionally loose and rocky

Other users: Equestrians
Canine compatibility: Leashed dogs permitted
Fees and permits: None required
Schedule: Sunrise to sunset
Map: USGS Malibu Beach, CA
Trail contact: Mountains Restoration Trust; (818) 591-1701

Finding the trailhead: From US 101, exit at Valley Circle Boulevard and head south for 1 mile until you reach Val Mar. Make a right onto Val Mar and continue until you intersect Mulholland Highway. Turn right onto Mulholland and go approximately 4 miles to a left turn onto Stunt Road. Travel 1 mile to a large dirt parking area on the right. The trailhead is on the east end of the lot. GPS N34 5.719'/ W118 38.922'

The Hike

The Cold Creek area of the Santa Monica Mountains is extremely rich with historical and natural features. Because of this, it is considered a place of major significance among many different user groups. Much of the area has been placed under preservation, thanks to land acquisitions by the University of California–Los Angeles and the Mountains Restoration Trust. In addition to preserving the area's natural state, both organizations share the goal of educating visitors of the historical and natural importance of the area.

Once inhabited by the Native American Gabrielino and Chumash tribes, artifacts dating back to 3000 B.C. have been found in the vicinity of Cold Creek. Obvious evidence of their activity can still be found today along the hike featured here, in the form of mortar holes ground into the sandstone bedrock. With the use of a pestle, the early inhabitants used the holes to grind acorns into meal. The abundance of mortar holes in the area confirms how crucial the acorn was to their diet.

With water flowing year-round in Cold Creek, the riparian canyon supports a wide population of birds and reptiles, as well as over 300 species of plants. The threatened horned lizard and mountain king snake reside here, as do an assortment of frogs, salamanders, and water bugs. Coyotes, bobcats, deer, and the occasional mountain lion help round out some of the other creatures that call this place home.

From the parking area, the trail wastes no time becoming interesting. You immediately descend into an oak-shaded corridor, passing sandstone bedrock dotted with the aforementioned mortar holes after a few hundred feet on the right. A little farther along, an even better example of the holes can be found to the left, at the foot of a large coast live oak. Only 30 feet from the trail, the site is still easy to miss, so keep your eyes peeled. Soon after, you cross Cold Creek and continue the beautiful descent toward the Yucca

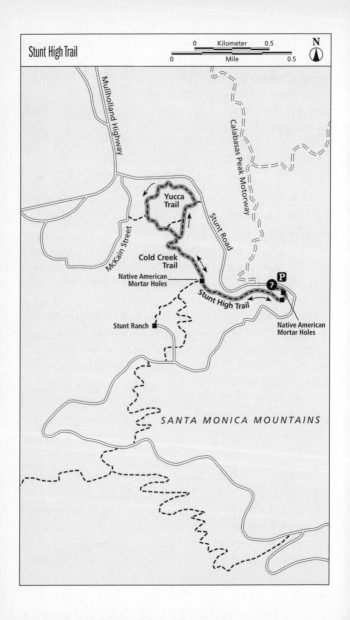

Stunt High Trail

0   Kilometer   0.5

0   Mile   0.5

N

Mulholland Highway

Calabasas Peak Motorway

Yucca Trail

Stunt Road

McKain Street

Cold Creek Trail

Native American Mortar Holes

Stunt High Trail

P

7

Native American Mortar Holes

Stunt Ranch

SANTA MONICA MOUNTAINS

Trail. There the shade from oaks and sycamores disappears as you loop through the Cold Creek Valley Preserve, surrounded mostly by chaparral.

Miles and Directions

0.0 From the dirt parking area, head east through the gate.

0.1 After crossing the first drainage, you come across Native American mortar holes in the sandstone to the right. A couple hundred feet farther down the trail, a small path leads 30 feet left to another mortar-hole site, at the base of an oak.

0.5 At the junction, the Stunt High Trail heads uphill to the left. Instead, go straight on the Cold Creek Trail. Mortar holes can be found in a large sandstone boulder to the left just before the junction. It is hidden by chaparral, but a short path leads up to it.

0.8 Trail crosses Cold Creek (walk across on stones) and shortly after intersects the Yucca Trail. Head right onto this trail.

1.0 After crossing a small drainage, head left at the intersection. Going right would take you 100 feet to Stunt Road.

1.3 When you reach the meadow, head left, easily stepping across an intermittent stream.

1.4 Veer left to follow the trail as it climbs a short, steep hill.

1.5 Head right at the minor junction to stay on the main trail. At the bottom of the hill, arrive back at Cold Creek Trail, completing the loop of the Cold Creek Valley Preserve. Return the way you came.

2.4 Arrive back at the parking area along Stunt Road.

8 Hummingbird Trail

Explore the otherworldly rock formations that adorn the hillsides below Rocky Peak with this engaging yet challenging hike. Gaining 1,000 feet of elevation in just over 2 miles, the difficulty is overshadowed by the geological wonders you will be eager to investigate along the way.

Distance: 4.6 miles out and back
Approximate hiking time: 3 hours
Best season: Oct–May
Difficulty: More challenging due to elevation gain
Trail surface: Dirt trail; rough and rocky in places
Other users: Equestrians and mountain bikers

Canine compatibility: Leashed dogs permitted
Fees and permits: None required
Schedule: Sunrise to sunset
Map: USGS Simi Valley East, CA
Trail contact: Rancho Simi Recreation and Park District; (805) 584-4400

Finding the trailhead: From the San Fernando Valley, head west on CA 118 to Simi Valley. Take the Kuehner Drive exit and turn right (north). After 0.1 mile, there is a dirt parking area to the right. Park here and follow the signs to the trailhead farther up Kuehner Drive. GPS N34 16.819'/W118 39.706'

The Hike

With 4,400 acres of rugged, boulder-strewn hills, the aptly named Rocky Peak Park separates the San Fernando and Simi Valleys. Particularly appealing to Western filmmakers, the Old West appearance of the area helped make it a popular setting for countless films, television shows, and commercials of all genres. Much of the area was formerly owned by Bob Hope, highlighting its ties to the entertainment industry.

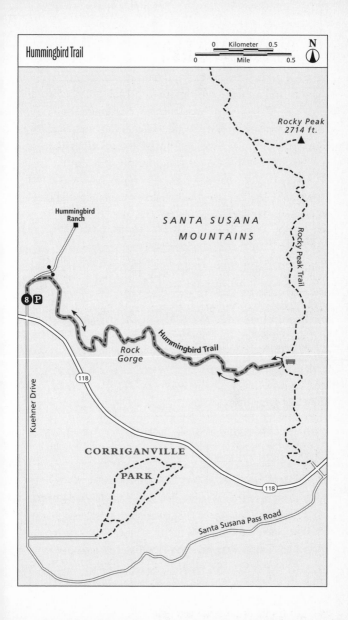

Hummingbird Trail

0 Kilometer 0.5
0 Mile 0.5

N

Rocky Peak
2714 ft. ▲

Hummingbird
Ranch ■

8 P

SANTA SUSANA
MOUNTAINS

Rocky Peak Trail

Hummingbird Trail

Rock
Gorge

Kuehner Drive

118

CORRIGANVILLE

PARK

118

Santa Susana Pass Road

Today the park entertains hikers, mountain bikers, and equestrians with numerous challenging trails. Almost all of the trails in the park share the theme of significant elevation gain, as well as being mostly out-and-back hikes. Making a loop out of these trails would require a significant amount of hiking on surface streets, and is generally avoided. Fortunately, the trails have enough noteworthy features along the way that they remain interesting on the return trip.

Named after the perennial Hummingbird Creek, the Hummingbird Trail is a popular hike leading up to the Rocky Peak Trail. About halfway up, the trail gives way to rock slabs reminiscent of the Navajo sandstone formations found in Utah and other southwestern states. Numerous caves can be found among the rock outcroppings along this section of trail, which offer a few moments' relief from the sun. With vegetation consisting mostly of coastal sage scrub, the rock formations will be the only source of shade along the trail after the morning hours. Fortunately, the trail becomes easier the higher you go, eventually arriving at a wooden bench at the intersection with the Rocky Peak Trail.

Miles and Directions

0.0 From the parking area, hike northeast along Kuehner Drive to the Hummingbird trailhead.

0.3 After descending into the ravine and heading south toward the freeway, the trail begins climbing eastward.

1.0 After several switchbacks, the trail heads into a rocky gorge.

1.5 More switchbacks are encountered before reaching a small plateau.

2.3 Trail concludes at the Rocky Peak Trail. Turn around here after enjoying the view.

4.6 Arrive back at the parking area along Kuehner Drive.

9 Porter Ranch Trails

Explore the wild side of Porter Ranch with this loop of atypical trails. Ranging from dirt roads and broken pavement to surface streets, the length and occasional steepness of this hike are sure to challenge, while the surroundings never let you forget where you are. Suburban hiking at its finest!

Distance: 6.1-mile lollipop
Approximate hiking time: 3 hours
Best season: Oct–June
Difficulty: Moderate
Trail surface: Well-traveled dirt roads with occasional surface streets
Other users: Equestrians and mountain bikers

Canine compatibility: Leashed dogs permitted
Fees and permits: None required
Schedule: Sunrise to sunset
Map: USGS Oat Mountain, CA
Trail contact: Aliso Canyon Park; (818) 756-8060

Finding the trailhead: From CA 118, exit at Reseda Boulevard and head north. Turn right on Rinaldi Street and look for the sign for Aliso Canyon Park on your left after 0.5 mile. There is no parking directly in front of the park, so proceed past the sign, make a U-turn, and park along the north side of Rinaldi. Follow the sidewalk west to the dirt road that descends north into the west side of the wash. GPS N34 16.742'/W118 31.583'

The Hike

Once the location of remote vacation homes and horse ranches owned by L.A.'s rich and famous, Porter Ranch now consists of a master-planned community of upscale suburban housing. It was the last portion of the San Fernando Valley to become developed, holding out until the

1970s. Fortunately, the equestrian roots of the area have been maintained, survived by a network of trails connecting various parts of the community with the neighboring hills and canyons. The trails serve local hikers and mountain bikers as well, providing a convenient, partial escape from suburban life.

The trails featured in this hike embody this convenience, albeit at the price of a purely natural setting. Almost nowhere along this hike will you witness nature untouched, for evidence of paving, grading, and various other construction necessities abound. Most of the trails utilize old roadbeds, with the exception of the Palisades Trail, which appears to have been built for the sole purpose of recreation. The 2-mile section of this trail between Tampa Avenue and Reseda Boulevard offers fantastic views of the Valley, and would make a worthwhile hike on its own.

Beginning with a stroll along Aliso Creek, the featured hike passes a native plant restoration area before a contrasting saunter over a graded hillside. Some effort is required to climb out of the canyon to the pavement of Sesnon Boulevard. Here a sidewalk cruise takes you to a shortcut across the grass-covered Porter Ridge Park, connecting with Ormskirk Avenue and the Sesnon Trail. This trail follows a dirt road behind multiple homes, with gas company land providing a border to the north. Eventually, the shade of Limekiln Canyon is reached, soon to be replaced by the exposed hillside traverse of the Palisades Trail and its steep decent back into Aliso Canyon.

Miles and Directions

0.0 From the west side of Aliso Canyon Wash, follow the dirt road north as it drops into the wash.

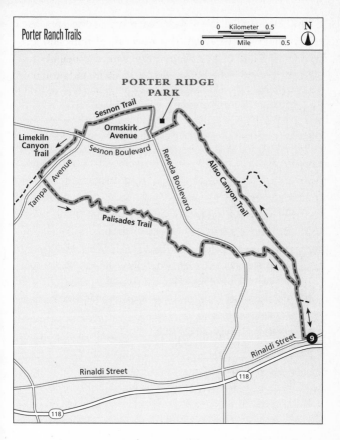

0 Kilometer 0.5

N

0 Mile 0.5

PORTER RIDGE PARK

Sesnon Trail

Ormskirk Avenue

Limekiln Canyon Trail

Sesnon Boulevard

Tampa Avenue

Reseda Boulevard

Aliso Canyon Trail

Palisades Trail

Rinaldi Street

9

Rinaldi Street

118

118

0.4 At the first major fork, bear right to cross the creek (use the rocks as stepping stones) and continue into shady Aliso Canyon.

1.6 Begin climbing steeply out of the canyon, ending at the paved dead end of Sesnon Boulevard. Follow the sidewalk west along Sesnon.

1.8 Turn north into Porter Ridge Park, passing the playground. Continue north up the sidewalk of Ormskirk Avenue.

2.1 At the dead end of Ormskirk, bear left (west) onto the Sesnon Trail. Follow it until it reaches the pavement of Tampa Avenue.

2.9 Take Tampa a short distance south to Sesnon Boulevard and turn right. After Sesnon crosses the wash, head south to pick up the Limekiln Canyon Trail as it drops into the shaded wash.

3.2 At the intersection of the paved road that leads up to Tampa, remain in the wash to stay on the Limekiln Canyon Trail.

3.3 At the next intersection, follow the dirt trail leading up to Tampa Avenue. Cross Tampa and climb the short paved road beyond the gate to pick up the Palisades Trail. Follow this lengthy trail as it traverses the hillside.

5.1 The Palisades Trail parallels Reseda Boulevard for 0.25 mile, heading south, before crossing it. There are signs for the trail on both sides of the street at this crossing.

5.7 Palisades Trail merges into the Aliso Canyon Trail, completing the loop.

6.1 Arrive back on Rinaldi Street.

10 Pierce College Cross-Country Trails

A true asset to residents of the San Fernando Valley, the Pierce College cross–country running trails border 240 acres of farmland, offering a convenient way to enjoy nature without leaving the city. Approximately 2 miles of publicly accessible dirt trails intertwine in the hills above the college, and options abound for customizing a hiking loop to your preference.

Distance: 2-mile loop, with several shorter options

Approximate hiking time: 1 hour

Best season: Year-round

Difficulty: Easy

Trail surface: Well-traveled dirt path

Other users: Runners

Canine compatibility: Dogs not allowed

Fees and permits: Parking is free on weekends. A permit is required most hours during the week and can be obtained at Parking Lot 7 for a fee.

Schedule: Sunrise to sunset

Map: Pierce College Campus Map

Trail Contact: Pierce College; (818) 347-0551; www.pierce college.edu

Finding the trailhead: From US 101, exit at Winnetka Avenue and head north. After approximately 1 mile, make a left on Brahma Drive. Continue down Brahma, and make a left onto Stadium Way. Head uphill on Stadium Way until you reach Parking Lot 4 on the left. Turn into the lot and park at the southernmost end. If you need to obtain a parking permit (the hours are set forth on the parking lot signs), continue on Stadium Way until you see Parking Lot 7 on the right. Turn into the lot and look for the parking permit dispensers at the south end. The permit is good for parking anywhere on campus, so you can return to Lot 4 and park as described above. GPS N34 10.887'/W118 34.716'

The Hike

As one of the last remaining farmlands in the San Fernando Valley, the Pierce College Farm seems out of place in an area so congested with urban expansion. At times under threat of development for more profitable uses, the farm serves as an agricultural laboratory for students, and is also a crucial habitat for migrating birds. Every spring the farm opens its doors to the public with their annual Farm Walk, allowing visitors to interact with the various animals that live there and witness firsthand what farm life is all about.

Another benefit of the farmland is that it makes the perfect setting for a cross-country running course. Widely popular among runners and hikers alike, the roughly 2-mile course snakes its way atop the hills overlooking the farmland. The trails lead past a red farmhouse surrounded by pepper trees and crisscross a picturesque hillside. The paths are smooth and well-maintained, and the hiking is very easy due to minor elevation changes. It is an excellent place to bring small children, since you can cut the loop short at almost any point along the trail and you are never more than 0.3 mile from the start. This fact also makes the hike perfect for those occasions when you only have a little time, but would like to get back to nature for a bit.

While the course may at times be marked with chalk, it is generally up to you to choose your route. To take in all of what the course has to offer, begin by heading northwest from the athletic field on the trail that climbs parallel to the parking lot. Continue straight at any junction until you descend to the gated road that leads to the farmhouse. From here, work your way back uphill on the interlaced trails, choosing whichever trail seems appealing to you.

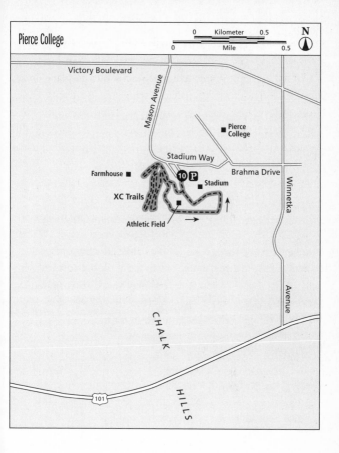

Eventually a couple of trails descend to the southern end of
the athletic field, and then climb up the moderately steep
hill across from it. From the top of this hill, a trail descends
into a grove of trees before looping back next to the football
stadium.

11 Rice Canyon and East Canyon Trails

Just over the Newhall Pass await these two spectacular canyon hikes. Physically right next to each other, the two routes share little in common aside from incredible scenery. The whole family can enjoy the fun hike up Rice Canyon, and those who want a further challenge can add the hike up East Canyon for a rewarding test of endurance.

Distance: 7.2 miles out and back

Approximate hiking time: 5 hours

Best season: Oct–May

Difficulty: Easy in Rice Canyon; more challenging in East Canyon due to continuous climbing

Trail surface: Well-traveled dirt trail or dirt road

Other users: Mountain bikers and equestrians

Canine compatibility: Leashed dogs permitted

Fees and permits: Small self-pay fee to park at trailhead

Schedule: Sunrise to sunset

Map: USGS Oat Mountain, CA

Trail contact: Mountains Recreation and Conservation Authority; (310) 589-3200

Finding the trailhead: From the Valley, take I-405 north until it merges with I-5. Take I-5 north over the Newhall Pass and exit at Calgrove Boulevard. Turn left on Calgrove and follow it south as it becomes The Old Road. After 1 mile, the parking area for Rice and East Canyons will be on the right. If you pass the first entrance, there is a second one a few hundred feet farther down the road. Free parking is also available along The Old Road. GPS N34 21.015'/W118 32.730'

The Hike

Situated in the undeveloped woodlands along I-5 at the Newhall Pass, East and Rice Canyons host a wide range of unique natural features. Most noticeable are the forests of Douglas fir trees growing at an unusually low elevation. They can be spotted by the keen eyes of drivers speeding along I-5, but are best appreciated up close by hiking along either canyon. In addition, California bay laurel and black walnut trees, plus three different species of oak, join the firs on the pastoral slopes of both canyons.

Not as obvious but just as amazing are the geological features of the area. Some of the oldest rocks in Southern California can be found nearby, dating back 1.7 billion years. Oil is in abundance under the hills, and natural oil seeps can be spotted within many of the canyons, including Rice. Nearby Pico Canyon was home to "CSO No. 4," a fruitful oil well that not only gave birth to the oil industry in California, but also was the longest-running oil well in the world.

The hike begins with a stroll up Rice Canyon. The trail splits time between verdant meadows and shaded stream crossings before climbing up to a grassy plateau. Here a giant fallen oak signifies the ideal spot to turn around. After returning to the bottom of the canyon, bear right to begin the trek up East Canyon. Contrary to the mellow grade of Rice Canyon, the East Canyon Trail is steeper and more sustained. However, the goal of this portion of the hike is to gain elevation, and soon enough you will be rewarded with excellent views of the Santa Clarita and San Fernando Valleys.

Miles and Directions

0.0 From the parking area, head west to a gated dirt road and begin following it south.

0.5 Reach signed junction of Rice Canyon and East Canyon. Bear right onto the Rice Canyon Trail.

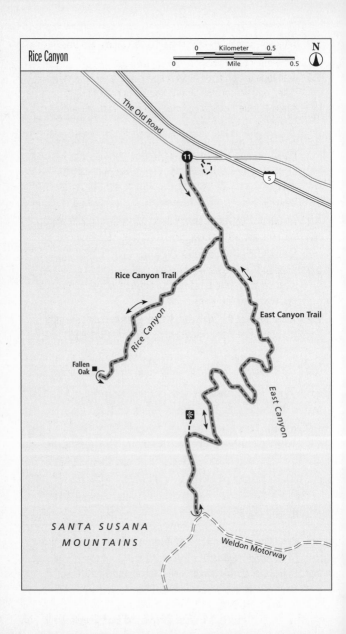

0   Kilometer   0.5

0   Mile   0.5

N

The Old Road

11

5

Rice Canyon Trail

East Canyon Trail

Rice Canyon

Fallen Oak

East Canyon

SANTA SUSANA MOUNTAINS

Weldon Motorway

1.2 After you step across the stream a few times, the trail begins climbing out of the canyon.

1.3 Trail tops out on a small shelf and heads over to a large fallen oak tree. A smaller trail continues straight up the steep hillside, dissipating into the brush. Instead, turn around at the fallen oak.

2.5 After hiking back down Rice Canyon, the junction with East Canyon is reached. (**Option:** Head left if you want to return to the trailhead and complete a shorter 3-mile hike.) To continue the featured hike, bear right (south) to explore East Canyon.

4.2 A spur trail branches off to the right and leads to an amazing overlook after a couple hundred feet. Continue up East Canyon Trail after having a look.

4.6 Weldon Motorway intersects East Canyon Trail from the left. After catching your breath and enjoying the view of the Valley, turn back the way you came.

7.2 Arrive back at the trailhead. If time permits, walk the informative nature loop, which begins in front of the main parking lot.

12 Caballero Canyon Trail

The Caballero Canyon Trail is a short canyon hike that follows a rocky streambed for about a mile before climbing up to the ridgeline of the Santa Monica Mountains. The trail ends at the famous ridge route known as Dirt Mulholland, which affords excellent views of the Valley as well as access to a great number of further hiking opportunities.

Distance: 3.2 miles out and back

Approximate hiking time: 2 hours

Best season: Oct–June

Difficulty: Moderate, with gradual climbing

Trail surface: Rocky streambed to well-traveled dirt trail

Other users: Mountain bikers

Canine compatibility: Leashed dogs permitted

Fees and permits: None required

Schedule: Sunrise to sunset

Map: USGS Canoga Park, CA

Trail contact: Santa Monica Mountains Conservancy; (310) 589-3200

Finding the trailhead: From US 101, take Reseda Boulevard south. After a couple miles and several stop signs, Reseda begins climbing uphill, passing a golf course on the left. Shortly thereafter, a sign for the trailhead will become visible on the left side of the road, opposite the entrance of the Braemar Country Club. Parking is available along both sides of Reseda. GPS N34 8.540'/W118 32.469'

The Hike

The Caballero Canyon Trail is one of the most popular trails in this book for many good reasons. Most obvious is the fact that it is conveniently located just off a major street in a well-developed portion of the Valley. Another reason is that it leads to a major artery of the Santa Monica Mountains trail system, Dirt Mulholland. With these two reasons alone, one doesn't even need to mention the beauty of Caballero Canyon and the intermittent stream flowing down it to justify the trail's popularity. Whatever the reason may be, this trail sees a lot of traffic.

As is the case with many of the hikes in this book, the Caballero Canyon Trail is most enjoyable in the late winter and spring, when the riparian habitat of the canyon is at its peak. During the summer months the canyon dries out and loses some of its allure, but the hike remains fun nonetheless, and the views from the top are always welcome.

It is worth mentioning that this hike can easily be done as a loop, walking westward on Dirt Mulholland to connect with the top of Reseda, but you would have to walk along the paved portion of Reseda for about a mile in order to return to your vehicle. Various other loop options exist for the more adventurous, but these hikes are beyond the context of this book.

The trail begins by descending into the wash, running parallel with Reseda. There is an unmarked trail that immediately heads across the wash and begins climbing, but for our route, stay to the right (west) of the wash for now. Due to the amount of traffic this trail sees, it is usually in very good condition and easy to follow. After about 1 mile you will exit the canyon and begin a steeper ascent on an old dirt road. The gradual climb continues to the obvious ridge ahead, whereupon Dirt Mulholland waits. Turn around here after taking in the spectacular view of the Valley.

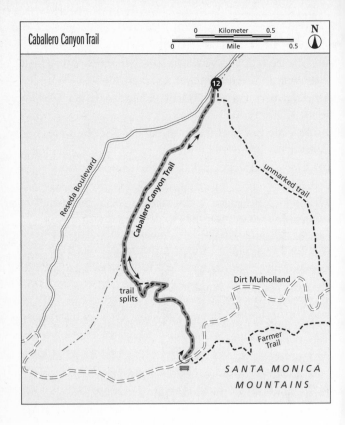

Caballero Canyon Trail

0　Kilometer　0.5
0　Mile　0.5

N

Reseda Boulevard

Caballero Canyon Trail

unmarked trail

trail splits

Dirt Mulholland

Farmer Trail

SANTA MONICA MOUNTAINS

Miles and Directions

0.0 Begin at the parking area on Reseda Boulevard.

0.4 Trail crosses an intermittent stream. It's easy to step across.

0.8 Trail veers into the canyon on left and begins climbing.

1.0 Trail splits in two for a few hundred feet before rejoining. The right option is less steep.

1.6 Trail concludes at Dirt Mulholland. Turn around here.

3.2 Arrive back at the trailhead.

13 Betty B. Dearing Trail

Beginning at the informative TreePeople facility in Cold-water Canyon Park, this pleasant loop explores a portion of the 128-acre Wilacre Park before meandering through the shaded suburbs of Studio City. From there, a dirt road traverses the opposite side of the canyon from Wilacre Park, completing the loop.

Distance: 2.8-mile loop
Approximate hiking time: 1.5 hours
Best season: Oct–June
Difficulty: Easy, with one steep, paved climb
Trail surface: Well-traveled dirt road, with some walking on surface streets

Other users: Dog walkers and mountain bikers
Canine compatibility: Leashed dogs permitted
Fees and permits: None required
Schedule: 6:30 a.m. to sunset
Map: USGS Van Nuys, CA
Trail contact: Santa Monica Mountains Conservancy; (310) 589-3200

Finding the trailhead: From US 101, take Coldwater Canyon Avenue south. Coldwater Canyon will eventually begin winding up into the hills. After approximately 2.5 miles from the freeway, arrive at a stoplight for the intersection with Mulholland Drive and Franklin Canyon Drive. Turn left just before this light into the parking lot for the TreePeople facility. GPS N34 7.736'/W118 24.395'

The Hike

This hike begins at the TreePeople headquarters, located atop the Santa Monica Mountains in Coldwater Canyon Park. TreePeople is a nonprofit environmental organization dedicated to restoring nature to our cities. Their goal is a mix of empowering communities to plant trees, educating children about the environment, and working with local government agencies on the critical issues that concern L.A. County's water supply. Their facility includes informative kiosks, a tree nursery, and a large outdoor amphitheater. Several short trails tour the grounds and lead over to Wilacre Park and the Betty B. Dearing Trail.

Named for the conservationist who fought for the completion of numerous trails in the Santa Monica Mountains, the Betty B. Dearing Trail probably sees more use than any other trail in this guide. If it is not raining, you will most likely come across other users on this trail. As the trail descends into Wilacre Park, it offers nice views of the Valley and the remaining undeveloped lands surrounding the area. Cypress, walnut, and pine trees provide ample shade for hot summer days on the final steep section of the descent. Here the trail turns to pavement, keeping it from becoming a muddy slip-and-slide during the wetter months.

Once Fryman Road is reached, the hike takes to the suburban streets of Studio City for just over 0.5 mile in order to reconnect with a section of the Betty B. Dearing Trail that leads back to TreePeople. This portion traverses the opposite side of Iredell Canyon from Wilacre Park, before intersecting the start of the loop below the Tree-People facility. If you didn't explore the terraces of short trails that line the TreePeople headquarters on the way in, be sure to do so before you leave.

Miles and Directions

0.0 Begin at the TreePeople headquarters parking area. Numerous options exist for the start. The most basic is to descend a staircase on the north end of the lot. At the bottom, head

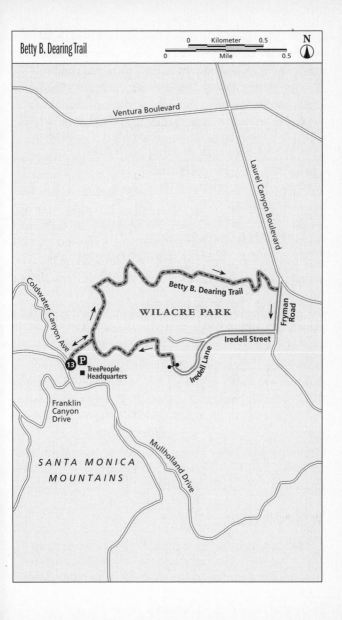

east a few steps, descend a second staircase, and then head east again.

0.2 The shady woodchip-covered trail ends at a T with the Betty B. Dearing Trail. Head left (north) for a short climb followed by a long descent.

1.6 Trail arrives at a large parking area on Fryman Road. You will now hike for about 0.5 mile on surface streets, so watch out for traffic. Head right (south) on Fryman Road.

1.7 Make a right onto Iredell Street.

2.0 Veer left onto Iredell Lane and begin a short, steep climb to the cul-de-sac.

2.2 Walk around the gate at the end of the cul-de-sac to pick up the Betty B. Dearing Trail again.

2.6 Arrive below the TreePeople facility, where a trail on the left ascends to the east end of the grounds; or you can return the way you came in.

2.8 Hike concludes at the TreePeople parking area.

14 O'Melveny Park

Take a stroll along citrus groves, grassy fields, and a riparian canyon in this tranquil park situated in Granada Hills. Finish with a respectable view of the San Fernando Valley, or continue with an optional 1.5 miles of demanding uphill trekking to the best view of the Valley in this book.

Distance: 5.6 miles out and back
Approximate hiking time: 4 hours
Best season: Oct–May
Difficulty: Easy first mile; more challenging on the Mission Point ascent
Trail surface: Well-traveled dirt roads or trails; some sections can be loose or overgrown

Other users: Equestrians and mountain bikers
Canine compatibility: Leashed dogs permitted
Fees and permits: None required
Schedule: Sunrise to sunset
Map: USGS Oat Mountain, CA
Trail contact: O'Melveny Park; (818) 368-5019

Finding the trailhead: From CA 118, exit at Balboa Boulevard and head north 2.3 miles to Sesnon Boulevard. Make a left on Sesnon, following it for just over 0.5 mile to the entrance of O'Melveny Park on the right. GPS N34 18.464'/W118 30.653'

The Hike

O'Melveny Park is L.A. County's second-largest park, yielding only to the expanses of Griffith Park on the opposite side of the Valley. Originally known as C. J. Ranch, the 672-acre park was once used to grow citrus fruits and raise cattle. Today, grapefruit trees line the entrance to the park, but little evidence remains of the erstwhile cattle-raising

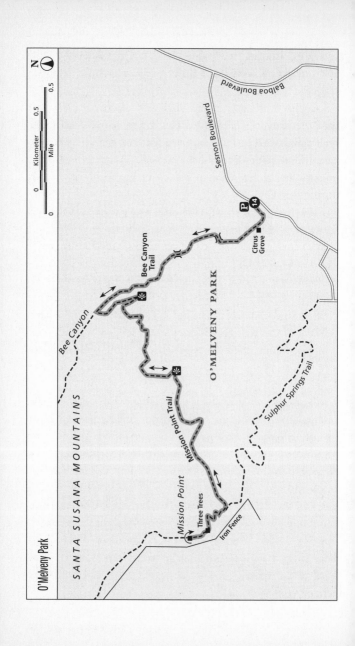

O'Melveny Park

activities. Instead, well-maintained lawns shaded by oaks and eucalyptus trees extend over a quarter-mile into Bee Canyon.

At the north end of the fields, a trail continues farther into the canyon, following Bee Canyon Creek. Although well-traveled, the trail can get a bit overgrown once you pass the Mission Point Trail turnoff. Also, since it later crosses the creek several times, it can become very muddy during the wet season.

The first 0.9 mile explores the initial section of the Bee Canyon Trail to the Mission Point Trail turnoff. The Mission Point Trail is then taken to its first overlook, whereupon you have the option of retracing your steps to the trailhead for an easy 2.2-mile hike. To get a better view of the Valley and a good workout, continue hiking up the challenging Mission Point Trail as far as you can. The latter portion of this trail climbs over 1,000 feet in 1.5 miles and is not recommended for beginners. It should definitely be avoided on hot days since there is virtually no shade to be found for most of the way.

However, if you are looking for a worthy test of your hiking fitness, you have come to the right place. You will be rewarded with increasingly better views the higher you go, until you reach the grandiose overlook at Mission Point. Arguably the best view of the Valley of all the hikes in this book, it comes at the heavy price of much exertion. The fact that the trail becomes partially overgrown and less obvious the higher you go gives testament to the high rate of attrition among hopeful climbers. Regardless of how high you make it, take comfort in the fact that it is all downhill back to the parking lot from any point along the climb; just retrace your steps.

Miles and Directions

0.0 From the parking lot, follow the paved road northwest as it heads into O'Melveny Park, passing a citrus grove on the left.

0.3 Paved path arrives at a fork. Head right, crossing a bridge over the creek, and follow the dirt road north.

0.4 Veer left at the next junction to stay in the canyon.

0.6 The various paths through the park converge before another bridge crossing, after which a single trail heads north into Bee Canyon. Follow this trail.

0.9 Arrive at the intersection with the Mission Point Trail. Head left up this gradual climb.

1.1 A nice overlook is reached to the south, while the trail switchbacks north and begins climbing steeply. (**Option:** Those who are looking for a leisurely outing should return to the Bee Canyon Trail after enjoying the view. There, you can continue north and follow the trail as far as you like before returning the same way, or simply retrace your steps back to the parking lot.) Those looking for a challenging hike should continue up the Mission Point Trail, referring to the mileages that follow.

1.8 After a short break in climbing, an overlook is reached, with views of the East Valley as well as downtown L.A.

2.1 Trail forks to the right to follow a steep firebreak.

2.5 Trail merges into the Sulphur Springs Trail. Follow the steep trail east of the iron fence as it switchbacks northward to the "Three Trees."

2.7 Pass the three large oak trees and follow another steep trail parallel to the fence up to Mission Point.

2.8 Arrive at the top of Mission Point. Retrace your steps after enjoying the view.

5.6 Arrive back at the O'Melveny Park parking area.

15 Stough Canyon

Beginning at the Stough Canyon Nature Center, this hike takes you on a scenic loop within the Verdugo Mountains. Though the trail begins steeply, the grade lessens throughout the ascent, making this trip suitable for most hikers. At the top of the climb, another trail descends the ridgeline back to the start, with incredible views along the way.

Distance: 2.7-mile lollipop
Approximate hiking time: 2 hours
Best season: Oct–May
Difficulty: Moderate due to elevation gain
Trail surface: Well-traveled dirt road or trail
Other users: Mountain bikers

Canine compatibility: Leashed dogs permitted
Fees and permits: None required
Schedule: Sunrise to sunset
Map: USGS Burbank, CA
Trail contact: Stough Canyon Nature Center; (818) 238-5440

Finding the trailhead: From I-5 in Burbank, exit at Burbank Boulevard and head east for 1 block. Turn left on San Fernando Boulevard and travel 2 blocks to a right turn at Delaware Road. Head 2 blocks down Delaware and turn right onto Glenoaks Boulevard. After 1 block on Glenoaks, turn left onto Walnut Avenue. Drive approximately 2 miles up Walnut until you reach the gated entrance to the Stough Canyon Nature Center, and park along the side of the road. If the gate is open, you can park farther up at the nature center. GPS N34 12.682'/W118 18.302'

The Hike

Rising high above the city of Burbank, the Verdugo Mountains form the eastern boundary of the San Fernando Valley.

Although dwarfed in size by the San Gabriel Mountains to the north and east, the chaparral-covered slopes of the Verdugos protrude steeply from the valley floor to a height of 3,126 feet, making them appear just as impressive. Despite their urban setting, the steep and rugged hillsides of the Verdugos conspire to preserve the area's natural state, as the range sees far less activity, both commercial and recreational, than the neighboring mountains.

Since the range is almost completely flanked by urban development, the Verdugo Mountains are essentially a wildlife island. Some of the animals marooned here include gray foxes, raccoons, coyotes, mule deer, and bobcats. Mountain lions are able to visit the hills by taking advantage of a partially urban 3-mile corridor through the Big Tujunga Wash, which extends into the San Gabriel Mountains. Their presence adds to the perception many people have of the Verdugos—that it is a wild and undeveloped place, unchanged over the centuries.

The hike begins at the Stough Canyon Nature Center, which is worth visiting if you are interested in learning about the habitat and natural history of the area. Its operating hours change depending on the season, so be sure to contact the center beforehand if you plan on visiting. The trailhead for the hike sits just west of the nature center, at the bottom of a moderately steep dirt road. This dirt road is the Stough Canyon Trail, and you will follow it up to the Verdugo Motorway. For the descent, the hike follows the narrow path of the Old Youth Camp Loop Trail, which has spectacular views of the city and passes by the ruins of a 1920s youth camp facility. Just before this trail rejoins the Stough Canyon Trail, an optional short climb up a dirt road takes you to an excellent viewing area.

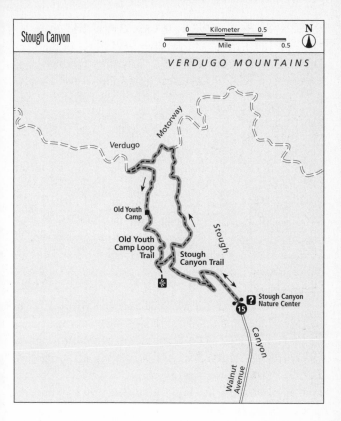

Stough Canyon

0 Kilometer 0.5
0 Mile 0.5

N

VERDUGO MOUNTAINS

Motorway

Verdugo

Old Youth
Camp

Old Youth
Camp Loop
Trail

Stough
Canyon Trail

Stough

Stough Canyon
Nature Center

15

Canyon

Walnut
Avenue

Miles and Directions

0.0 Hike begins at the top of Walnut Avenue, just before the entrance gate to the Stough Canyon Nature Center. Hike past the gate and up the sidewalk.

0.2 Paved sidewalk reaches the facility and the trailhead for the Stough Canyon Trail. Head up the dirt road beyond the trailhead.

0.3 Bear right at the switchback to stay on the obvious main trail.

0.6 Head right at the junction with the Old Youth Camp Loop Trail, staying on the Stough Canyon Trail.

1.2 Stough Canyon Trail tops out at the Verdugo Motorway. Head left on this dirt road.

1.4 Reach junction with the Old Youth Camp Loop Trail. Head left up this narrow trail.

1.7 Trail passes the ruins of the Old Youth Camp area.

2.0 Take the left fork to continue the descent. (**Option:** Head straight up a short hill to an excellent viewing area.)

2.1 Old Youth Camp Loop Trail concludes at the Stough Canyon Trail. Retrace this road back to the trailhead.

2.7 Arrive back at the parking area on Walnut Avenue.

16 Griffith Park Trails with Amir's Garden

Located within the hills of Griffith Park, this hike begins with a climb to the lovely Amir's Garden and then follows several equestrian trails to make a pleasant loop. While the views will remind you that you are in an urban park, the hike is surprisingly tranquil, offering refuge from the city as well as a chance to explore the beauty of the garden.

Distance: 2.6-mile loop
Approximate hiking time: 2 hours
Best season: Oct–June
Difficulty: Moderate due to some short, steep climbs and descents
Trail surface: Well-traveled dirt road
Other users: Equestrians
Canine compatibility: Leashed dogs permitted

Fees and permits: None required
Schedule: 5:00 a.m. to sunset
Maps: USGS Burbank, CA; Hileman's Recreational & Geological Map of Griffith Park
Trail contact: Griffith Park; (323) 913-4688; www.laparks.org/dos/parks/griffithpk

Finding the trailhead: Heading westbound on CA 134, exit at Forest Lawn Drive and go south for about 500 feet to Zoo Drive. Make a left at Zoo Drive and proceed to the intersection with Griffith Park Drive. Turn right onto Griffith Park Drive and travel 1.5 miles to the southeast corner of the Mineral Wells Picnic Area. Parking is located here on Mineral Wells Drive, just after a right turn at the stop sign. GPS N34 8.702'/W118 17.629'

The Hike

Thanks to the unique geography surrounding Los Angeles and the San Fernando Valley, Griffith Park is the largest municipal park with urban wilderness in the United States. The park consists of more than 4,210 acres of both natural and landscaped terrain, and it is home to many diverse recreational activities and attractions.

One of the lesser-known attractions is Amir's Garden, a wonderful garden oasis perched atop a hillside overlooking Los Angeles. Here a terraced network of shady pathways traverses the garden, and numerous benches provide spots to relax and contemplate the surrounding beauty. Established in 1971 by Amir Dialameh, an immigrant from Iran, the garden is a testament to his belief in American values and the effects that one person can have on his or her community. Although Amir passed away in 2003, the five-acre garden is still maintained by volunteers who share his vision. To learn more, visit www.amirsgarden.org.

The hike begins with a climb up to Amir's Garden. While the dirt road leading to the garden is steep in the beginning, the grade becomes easier the farther you go. Once you reach the garden, the trail switchbacks west and continues to climb for another 0.5 mile. You will soon be above the not-so-scenic Toyon Canyon Land Reclamation Project. This area served as a garbage dump for the city of Los Angeles from 1957 to 1985, though not without a lot of opposition. Hopefully, the land will one day be reconditioned and used for purposes better suited to the park in which it lies.

After circumnavigating the landfill site, you will probably notice that you are hiking on a well-established equestrian

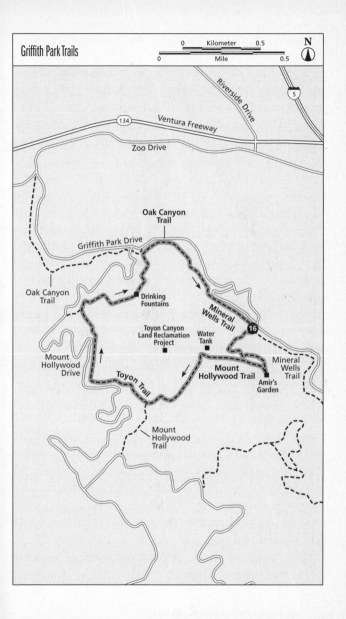

Griffith Park Trails

N

0   Kilometer   0.5
0   Mile   0.5

Riverside Drive

5

134   Ventura Freeway

Zoo Drive

Oak Canyon
Trail

Griffith Park Drive

Oak Canyon
Trail

Drinking
Fountains

Toyon Canyon
Land Reclamation
Project

Water
Tank

Mineral
Wells Trail

16

Mount
Hollywood
Drive

Toyon Trail

Mount
Hollywood Trail

Mineral
Wells
Trail

Amir's
Garden

Mount
Hollywood
Trail

trail. If this wasn't yet obvious to you, the horse drinking fountains at mile 1.7 should make it clear. If you are thirsty, be sure to use the human versions also located there.

Along this portion of trail are bushes of the endangered Nevin's barberry. This native shrub produces bright red berries during the summer months, and while the berries are edible, you may need to use the above-mentioned drinking fountain to wash down their sour lemon taste.

After some moderate downhill hiking, the bustle of Griffith Park returns to your consciousness as you travel parallel to Griffith Park Drive on the busy Oak Canyon Trail. The trend continues as you merge onto the Mineral Wells Trail, which is a pleasant, shady path, taking you back to the parking area.

Miles and Directions

0.0 From the Mineral Wells Picnic Area parking lot, head to the southeast junction of Griffith Park Drive and Mineral Wells Drive. From here, begin climbing the moderately steep dirt road that ascends west.

0.4 Dirt road comes to a sharp right switchback, with Amir's Garden straight ahead. After exploring the garden, return to the switchback and continue up the dirt road.

0.6 A small dirt road branches off to the right, leading to a water tank. Continue straight on the main trail.

0.7 Trail reaches a T. Bear left and continue uphill.

0.9 Trail forks to the right at a large eucalyptus tree.

1.0 Toyon Trail turns off from the main dirt road and descends to the right, noted by a black-and-white-striped pole. Be sure to make this crucial right turn.

1.2 Trail passes a construction yard on its western side. Follow the equestrian trail signs.

1.6 Trail merges with an unmarked trail. Continue downhill.

2.1 Toyon Trail ends at the Oak Canyon Trail. Take a right onto this trail.

2.4 Oak Canyon Trail becomes Mineral Wells Trail after crossing cement drainage.

2.6 Hike finishes at the Mineral Wells Picnic Area parking area. Restrooms are available here.

17 Musch Trail to Eagle Rock

In the coastal woodlands surrounding Topanga Canyon, networks of excellent hiking trails lead to unique natural features. This loop hike explores the grassy meadows and riparian canyons common to the area, finishing with a visit to the popular sandstone formation known as Eagle Rock.

Distance: 4.5-mile loop
Approximate hiking time: 3 hours
Best season: Oct–May
Difficulty: Moderate, with some sustained climbing
Trail surface: Well-traveled dirt trail or road
Other users: Equestrians; mountain bikers on the dirt roads

Canine compatibility: Dogs not permitted
Fees and permits: Moderate parking fee Schedule: 8:00 a.m. to dusk
Map: USGS Topanga, CA
Trail contact: Topanga State Park; (310) 455-2465
Special considerations: Rattlesnakes are common during the summer months.

Finding the trailhead: From US 101, exit at Topanga Canyon Boulevard and head south. Follow this road approximately 8 miles into Topanga Canyon to a left turn onto Entrada Road. Continue up Entrada for 1 mile, following the signs to Topanaga State Park and the Trippet Ranch parking area. You can park along Entrada to avoid the parking fee at Trippet Ranch. GPS N34 5.605'/W118 35.277'

The Hike

Topanga State Park is considered to be the world's largest wildland inside the boundaries of a major city, since it is located entirely within the city limits of Los Angeles. Despite this designation, only 36 miles of dirt roads and trails traverse the parkland's 11,000 acres, leaving most of the terrain in its natural state. While the trails can be busy at times, Topanga State Park provides a great backcountry experience and will evoke feelings of remoteness once you forget about the surrounding metropolis.

This hike has several attributes that make it unique to the other hikes in this book. The most obvious feature is that the loop provides the only close-up views of the Pacific Ocean. On a clear day, you will have an unobstructed view of Catalina Island and the Palos Verdes Peninsula, with the bench at Eagle Rock providing the perfect vantage point.

Another distinguishing trait of this hike is that it passes through an established hike-in campground, a rarity within the Santa Monica Mountains. Musch Camp is a first-come, first-served campsite set among the shade of numerous nonnative eucalyptus trees. Campgrounds such as this are common in the Angeles National Forest, but only one other exists in the Santa Monica Mountains. This campground would be particularly well-suited for those who wish to hike the entire length of the Backbone Trail in one outing—which brings us to the third unique characteristic of this hike.

The Backbone Trail System has been in the making for over fifty years. The goal during this time has been to create a trail system that traverses the entire range of the Santa Monica Mountains, favoring ridgelines and areas of natural interest. By linking existing and newly constructed trails, the Backbone Trail System will be approximately 70 miles long when it is completed. At the time of this writing, 65 miles have been completed, with the featured hike traversing 2.5 miles of it. All of the Musch Trail, and the north portion of the Eagle Springs Fire Road, combine to make up a short

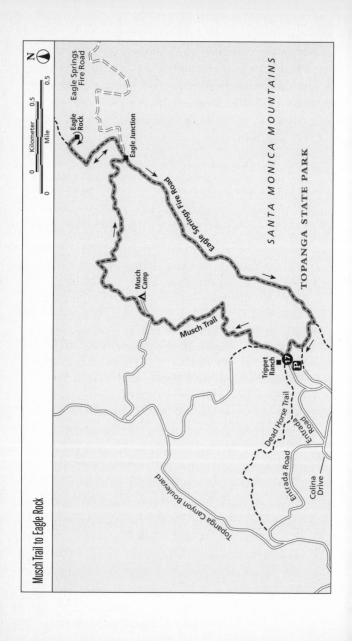

Musch Trail to Eagle Rock

Eagle Springs Fire Road

Eagle Rock

Eagle Junction

Eagle Springs Fire Road

Musch Camp

Musch Trail

SANTA MONICA MOUNTAINS

TOPANGA STATE PARK

Trippet Ranch

17 P

Dead Horse Trail

Entrada Road

Colina Drive

Topanga Canyon Boulevard

N

Kilometer   0   0.5

Mile   0   0.5

segment of the Backbone Trail. Beginning at Will Rogers State Historic Park and finishing at Point Mugu State Park, the completion of the Backbone Trail will be a great victory for trail users all over Southern California.

Miles and Directions

0.0 From the northeast corner of the Trippet Ranch parking lot, the signed Musch Trail begins on a paved service road and passes a pond on the right.

0.1 Veer right off the service road onto the signed dirt path.

0.7 Trail passes a wooden bench overlooking Topanga Canyon.

0.9 Head right (east) at the junction, following the Musch Trail signs. Soon you will pass through Musch Camp.

2.1 Musch Trail concludes at Eagle Junction. Turn left onto the north loop of Eagle Springs Fire Road, following the signs for Eagle Rock.

2.6 Arrive at the Eagle Rock turnoff. Head up the short trail to the right to a wooden bench overlooking the Pacific Ocean. Use caution if you decide to climb to the top of Eagle Rock. Turn around here after you have taken in the beautiful views of the Valley and the ocean.

3.0 Once you arrive back at Eagle Junction, continue heading straight on the dirt road for the return trip down Eagle Springs Fire Road.

4.4 Veer right to follow the wide dirt road down to the parking area.

4.5 Arrive back at the Trippet Ranch parking area.

18 Mendenhall Ridge Road

High atop the foothills of the San Gabriel Mountains, this secluded dirt road traverses the southern ridge above Pacoima Canyon. Along the way, you pass through oak and Douglas fir groves before arriving at Highline Saddle, where you are rewarded with a detached view of the Valley from the highest elevation in this book.

Distance: 5.2 miles out and back
Approximate hiking time: 3 hours
Best season: Oct–May
Difficulty: Moderate due to length
Trail surface: Well-traveled dirt road
Other users: Equestrians and mountain bikers

Canine compatibility: Leashed dogs permitted
Fees and permits: None required
Schedule: Always open
Map: USGS Sunland, CA
Trail contact: Los Angeles River Ranger District Office; (818) 899-1900

Finding the trailhead: From the Valley, head east on CA 118 and merge onto I-210 east. Take the Osborne Street exit and turn left (north) onto Foothill Boulevard. After 1 block, make another left onto Osborne Street. After about 1 mile, Osborne Street becomes Little Tujunga Canyon Road and begins winding up into the foothills. Approximately 7.3 miles from the freeway, you reach a high point known as the Dillon Divide. Park on the right in a dirt pullout just before the road begins to descend. To the right is the closed gate for Forest Road 3N32 and the start of this hike. GPS N34 20.682'/ W118 20.971'

The Hike

Despite their close proximity to the metropolis, the west-

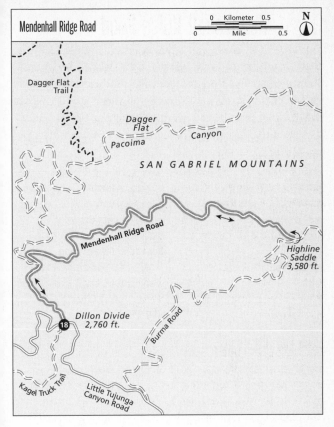

0   Kilometer   0.5
0   Mile   0.5

N

Dagger Flat
Trail

Dagger
Flat
Canyon

Pacoima

SAN GABRIEL MOUNTAINS

Mendenhall Ridge Road

Highline
Saddle
3,580 ft.

Dillon Divide
2,760 ft.

18

Burma Road

Kagel Truck Trail

Little Tujunga
Canyon Road

ernmost portion of the San Gabriel Mountains sees relatively light recreational use. While the foothills that border the northeast Valley are popular among equestrians, the trails they use tend to be short, dusty loops that are not very enjoyable for hiking. A few miles' drive up one of the few canyon roads, however, will find you in seclusion among the chaparral-covered mountains, where several decent hiking opportunities exist.

Mendenhall Ridge Road begins along the only paved road that bisects this part of the range, at a place known as Dillon Divide, elevation 2,760 feet. Named after William V. Mendenhall, the Angeles National Forest supervisor from 1929 to 1957, the ridge itself extends about 12 miles from Dillon Divide eastward toward Mount Gleason. Along the way, it gradually gains more than 3,000 feet of elevation.

The hike featured here explores the first 2.6 miles of this road, which culminates at the Highline Saddle, elevation 3,580 feet. The dirt road traverses the north side of the ridge, which affords views into Pacoima Canyon as well as welcome shade for much of the way. Despite the availability of shade, this area can still become incredibly hot during the summer. Conversely, it is not uncommon to see patches of snow alongside portions of the road during winter. Either way, the ease of hiking combined with the noncommittal nature of the route make this hike a good option any time of year—just be sure to dress appropriately.

Miles and Directions

- **0.0** From the dirt pullout alongside Little Tujunga Canyon Road, begin hiking east on the dirt road beyond the gate that is marked Forest Road 3N32.
- **0.5** A smaller dirt road forks to the left and descends into Pacoima Canyon. Continue straight on the main dirt road, climbing gradually.
- **1.2** Dirt road passes by several large Douglas fir trees.
- **2.6** Highline Saddle is reached, and you finally have a view of the San Fernando Valley. Turn around here after enjoying the view.
- **5.2** Arrive back at Little Tujunga Canyon Road.

19 Trail Canyon Falls

A year-round waterfall is somewhat rare in the hills surrounding the Valley, especially one as large and accessible as Trail Canyon Falls. This pleasant hike up a stream-lined canyon to the majestic 50-foot waterfall serves as a great introduction to the hiking found within the Angeles National Forest.

Distance: 3.2 miles out and back

Approximate hiking time: 2.5 hours

Best season: Oct–June

Difficulty: Moderate, with some sustained uphill hiking

Trail surface: Well-traveled dirt road or trail; several creek crossings

Other users: Equestrians

Canine compatibility: Leashed dogs permitted

Fees and permits: National Forest Adventure Pass required for parking; day pass or annual pass available at ranger station

Schedule: Always open

Map: USGS Sunland, CA

Trail contact: Los Angeles River Ranger District; (818) 899-1900

Finding the trailhead: From I-210 heading east in Sunland, exit at Sunland Boulevard and turn left (east). Sunland becomes Foothill Boulevard. After 1.5 miles, turn left onto Mt. Gleason Avenue. After another 1.5 miles and several stop signs, Mt. Gleason ends at Big Tujunga Canyon Road. Turn right here and follow this road approximately 3.5 miles to Trail Canyon Road (an unmarked dirt road) on the left, just before a sign for the turnoff for Delta Flats. Proceed northeast up this dirt road, bearing right at the fork, to the parking area. GPS N34 18.321'/W118 15.315'

The Hike

Established in 1907, the Angeles National Forest has much to offer those who seek an outdoor wilderness experience close to home. Encompassing most of the San Gabriel Mountains, as well as parts of neighboring ranges, it makes a perfect setting for year-round recreation. Elevations range from 1,200 feet to over 10,000 feet, with activities such as hiking, fishing, mountain biking, backpacking, and skiing all just a short drive from the Valley.

Trail Canyon has been home to outdoor recreation for at least as long as the park has existed, thanks to its convenient location and scenic beauty. During the 1920s several cabins were built at the base of the canyon under special-use permits, and many are still in use today. Farther up the canyon are several primitive campsites that can accommodate overnight hikers. Like the rest of the San Gabriel Mountains, this area is steeped in history, which adds to the allure of this canyon hike.

After a rough dirt-road drive to the parking area (passable by two-wheel-drive vehicles except after heavy rains), the trail follows a dirt access road past several cabins. Eventually a narrow trail turns north from this road, following the creek bottom under the shade of cottonwood, alder, and sycamore trees. Several water crossings are encountered, aided by the use of stepping stones or logs placed by previous visitors.

Soon the trail leaves the stream bottom to climb and traverse the exposed hillside west of it. There is no shade along this stretch, so be sure to come prepared if the weather is hot. After this traverse and a sharp eastward bend, the top of Trail Canyon Falls comes into view on the right. From the main trail it is hard to get a full view of the falls, but several spur trails can be followed to get a closer look. These spur trails can be a bit treacherous, so be sure to use caution if you decide to approach the falls.

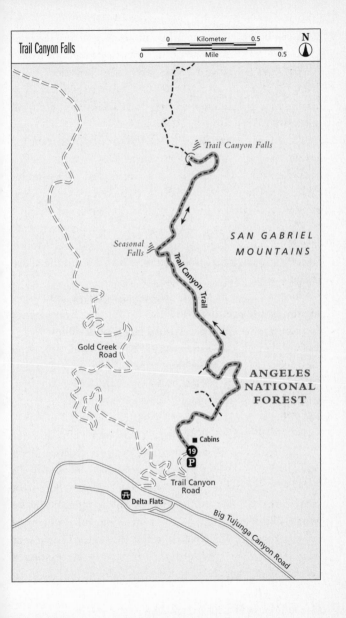

Trail Canyon Falls

Kilometer

0   0.5
Mile
0   0.5

N

Trail Canyon Falls

SAN GABRIEL
MOUNTAINS

Seasonal
Falls

Trail Canyon Trail

Gold Creek
Road

ANGELES
NATIONAL
FOREST

Cabins

19 P

Trail Canyon
Road

Delta Flats

Big Tujunga Canyon Road

Miles and Directions

0.0 From the parking area, head north to the trailhead and follow the dirt road past the closed gate. A few hundred feet
later, the trail forks left from the road, following the stream.

0.1 Trail merges back into the dirt road.

0.3 Head straight uphill at the intersection with a smaller dirt
road.

0.6 Traces of old pavement are crossed.

0.7 Turn right (north) off the dirt road to follow a narrow trail
as it heads upstream. Along the way, the trail crosses the
stream several times on stones and logs.

1.2 Trail leaves the canyon floor and begins climbing along the
west hillside. A 25-foot seasonal waterfall lies hidden in a
gully just west of the initial climb.

1.6 Trail Canyon Falls come into view after a long, exposed hillside traverse. Turn around here after enjoying the view.

3.2 Hike concludes at the parking area.

Clubs and Trail Groups

Mountains Restoration Trust
3815 Old Topanga Canyon Road
Calabasas, CA 91302
(818) 591-1701
www.mountainstrust.org
A nonprofit organization dedicated to preserving the wilderness land within the Santa Monica Mountains. It offers docent-led nature walks around the Cold Creek Watershed area as well as other educational programs.

Rancho Simi Trailblazers
(805) 584-4440
www.simitrailblazers.com
An organization of outdoor enthusiasts involved in trail maintenance, promotion, and preservation. The group sponsors weekly hikes for all abilities, in addition to trail maintenance days and monthly meetings.

Santa Monica Mountains Conservancy
(310) 589-3200
(323) 221-8900
www.smmc.ca.gov
The premier organization helping to acquire, manage, and conserve the wildlands in this portion of Southern California.

www.lamountains.com
This Web site, provided by the Santa Monica Mountains Conservancy, contains plenty of information on trails, events, and volunteer opportunities.

www.latrails.com

As the name suggests, this site focuses on providing trail information for hikes surrounding Los Angeles.

www.localhikes.com

This site provides information on hikes near metropolitan areas within the United States.

About the Author

Deke Williams is an avid outdoorsman who enjoys spending his free time hiking, mountain biking, and rock climbing in the wilds of Southern California. A native of Los Angeles, he is grateful to have grown up in an area of abundant year-round outdoor activities. Currently working in the electronics industry, he calls Westlake Village, California, home.